Handmade Tiles

Handmade Tiles

- Designing
- Making
- Decorating

Frank Giorgini

Lark Books

Editor: Chris Rich
Art Director: Kathleen Holmes
Production: Elaine Thompson and Kathleen Holmes
Illustrations: Don Osby
Photography of steps and techniques: Bobby Hansson

Library of Congress Cataloging-in-Publication Data
Giorgini, Frank, 1947–
    Handmade tiles : designing, making, decorating / by Frank Giorgini.
        p.   cm.
    Includes index.
    ISBN 0-937274-76-3 : $24.95
    1. Pottery craft.   2. Tiles.   I. Title.
TT920.G56   1994
738.6--dc20   94-15445
                                               CIP

10 9

Published in 1994 by Lark Books
50 College Street
Asheville, NC 28801
U.S.A.

For information about distribution in the U.S., Canada, the U.K., Europe, and Asia,
call Lark books at 828-253-0467.

Distributed in Australia by Capricorn Link (Australia) Pty Ltd., P.O. Box 6651,
Baulkham Hills Business Centre, NSW 2153, Australia

Distributed in New Zealand by Southern Publishers Group, 22 Burleigh St., Grafton,
Auckland, NZ

Printed in Hong Kong by Oceanic Graphic Printing

ISBN 0-937274-76-3

Cover tiles: Frank Giorgini. 1993
Hand-pressed from plaster mold
Model was sculpted from moist clay
Lettering done with layering technique
Photograph by Bobby Hansson

Title page: Frank Giorgini.
Afro Tile. 1992
12" x 12" (30.5 x 30.5 cm)
Photograph by Bobby Hansson

Opposite page: Frank Bosco
Close Corners. 1992
85" x 46" x 2" (215.9 x 116.8 x 5.1 cm)
Photograph by Dana Salvo

CONTENTS

INTRODUCTION

What is it about ceramic tiles that is so alluring and so comforting? For some people, it may be their permanence. Tiles have existed since the times of the Roman Empire and the Babylonians. For others, the sight of a tile may recall wonderful childhood memories of standing in a warm kitchen or lying in a steaming bath. Tiles certainly tend to linger, not just in our memories but in actual space as well. Unlike wallpaper or paint, they aren't replaced frequently. The shapes and images that are frozen in time on their surfaces can create an environment that affects generations to come.

Whatever their charm for individuals, the appeal of tiles spans the globe. Every culture with the technology and resources to do so has produced ceramic tiles. The levels of technology vary, of course, from hand-dug clay slabs, dried in the sun and fired with old automobile tires, to colossal factories hydraulically dust-pressing thousands of tiles per hour around the clock.

Clay has been my preferred medium in artistic expression for over twenty years. Although it's relatively valueless in its raw state, clay can be transformed by the human hand into objects of enduring beauty. And the process of shaping it is wonderfully practical and direct. This abundant material, so inviting to the touch, is completely malleable. It has no grain or direction and can be squeezed, pushed, scraped, paddled, and molded into almost any imaginable shape—from utilitarian vessels to sculptural objects and from decorative surfaces to musical instruments.

There is something very satisfying about working with clay. As you shape it, you "touch the earth." Through the miracle of hand, heart, and mind, you literally make something from nothing. My students at Parsons School of Design, where I've taught ceramic tile design and fabrication courses since 1985, include matriculated undergraduates in art and design, professionals in other disciplines of the art field, and people with no previous experience in art or clay. All of them, however, enjoy being able to express themselves with this user-friendly material. When they make a mistake, they just wad the clay back up and start again.

You don't need an art background to make tiles. In fact, some of the most exciting tiles in my classes come from students without one. People who get caught up in trying to make a tile that is "good art" often produce work that is contrived and lacking in vitality. If you can open up, instead, and express yourself from within, you will probably do very well.

My purpose in this book is to provide you with the techniques necessary to transform your images and ideas into the ceramic tile format. Once you've been introduced to the history of handmade tiles (in Chapter 1, written by Joseph Taylor of the Tile Heritage Foundation), you'll find that the chapter arrangement is based on the stages of the tile-making process. Descriptions of kilns, raw clay, tools, and studio space come first. Subsequent chapters extend from the process of shaping moist, malleable clay, fresh out of the bag, all the way to installing your finished work. Making relief tiles, decorating both unfired and bisque-fired clay, and firing your tiles, are all explained in detail. In addition, I've included chapters on mosaics, tile design, and health and safety, and—for readers who are handy in the workshop—instructions for making your own tools, including a studio tile press.

I address many methods of surface decoration, but my forte is the sculpting and handforming of clay tiles, and my emphasis is on the actual process of handmaking tiles. The step-by-step process for making relief tiles from plaster press molds is one of the tile-making methods that this book covers in detail. Transforming an amorphous lump of earthen material into a three-dimensional representation of my concept and vision is my idea of a good time.

Because I'm used to working with students whose experience and skill levels range from expert to nonexistent, I've tried to use the same teaching methods here—and to cover the same techniques—as I do in my classroom. It's therefore my hope that this book will be both a practical introduction for the novice and a valuable resource for the professional ceramist.

CHAPTER ONE

THE HANDCRAFTED TRADITION IN CERAMIC TILES

by Joseph A. Taylor

Opposite page:
Bernadette Stillo
Celebrate Life.
1993
5-3/4" x 7-3/4"
(14.6 x 19.7 cm)
Photograph by Bobby Hansson

Tile depicting Vernal Falls in Yosemite National Park. Claycraft Potteries, Los Angeles, California, circa 1926. Tile Heritage Foundation. Gift of Bart Huffman.

Sixteenth-century "cuenca" tiles. From the Museo Nacional de Cerámica Gonzalez Marti, Valencia, Spain. © Instituto de Promoción Cerámica, Castellón, Spain.
Photograph by Jorge Crespo

Late fourteenth-century tile work in the Alhambra (Granada, Spain). Patio de los Arrayanes. © Instituto de Promoción Cerámica, Castellón, Spain.
Photograph by Algara/Garrido

Today, more often than not, we think of ceramic tiles primarily as functional objects. For very practical reasons—tiles are durable and easy to maintain—we use them in our kitchens and bathrooms and on various floors throughout our homes. Characterized by their size, shape, color, and design, tiles nonetheless possess a particular beauty, one which is only a secondary consideration. Historically, however, this has not been the case. Although the function of tiles has been significant, aesthetics has played a major role in the development of ceramic tiles through the ages.

It doesn't take much imagination to envision ancient man forming his first tile out of moist earth and allowing it to dry in the sun. These early tiles were produced for use as paving materials and building blocks. Probably because their wet clay surfaces were so susceptible to accidental markings, tiles naturally became an early medium for communication and artistic expression.

Archaeologists continue to excavate bits and pieces of both pottery and tiles—shards that date back thousands of years—from sites around the world. When fired tiles were first produced and where the first tiles were installed are questions that may never be answered. Throughout the history of civilization, however, there have been periods during which tiles emerged and flourished primarily as a decorative medium, one influenced by social, political, and economic forces as well as by the technology at hand.

Many palaces and public buildings of the ancient world were adorned with tiles. Small, brightly colored, blue tiles were used to decorate the interior of the tomb of King Zoser of Egypt (2630-2611 B.C.) in the stepped pyramid at Sakkara. And in later years, the Assyrian Palace of Sargon at Khorsabad (722-705 B.C.), the imposing Ishtar Gate built by Nebuchadnezzar II in Babylon (604-562 B.C.), and the palaces of King Darius

at Susa and Persepolis in ancient Persia (521-486 B.C.) all included impressive tile work.

Through the millenniums, the development and proliferation of decorative tiles were influenced by a number of factors. One of these was movement along major land and sea trade routes, which encouraged the exchange of ideas and materials, especially where these routes intersected. Similarly, wars, political unrest, and religious fervor all played their part in the blending of cultures and in the subsequent artistic output in any given part of the world. When Islamic warriors overran the territories of the Near and Middle East (a period which began in the seventh century), for example, their leaders were irresistibly attracted to the artistic accomplishments of the peoples they conquered. These men adopted a keen appreciation for color and design, which they soon carried with them into Turkey, across North Africa, and eventually into Spain.

Although countless architectural masterpieces have been lost or relegated in part to museums for safekeeping, many examples of magnificent tile work still exist in situ. Some of the most breathtaking in both color and design are located in the Royal Palace of Shah Abbas I (1587-1629) in Isfahan (in present-day Iran), as well as in that city's spectacular mosques and mausoleums. Beautiful ceramic tiles are also found in the Blue Mosque in Istanbul, a structure designed by Sedefkar Mehmet Aga for Sultan Ahmet I and built between 1609 and 1617; this high degree of ceramic splendor has yet to be surpassed.

Since ancient times, skilled craftsmen—both tile makers and installers—have been respected members of many societies. Artisans were often employed by the governments of their countries and would travel to various centers of commerce and wealth in order to practice their skills. Over time, as these traveling tile makers

Spectacular tiles decorate the interior of the Blue Mosque in Istanbul.
Courtesy of Kalebodur Seramik Sanayi, A.S.

Detail of tile panel between windows in Ramazan Efendi Mosque, Istanbul. Courtesy of
Kalebodur Seramik Sanayi A.S.
Photo by Nuri Bilge Ceylan

Sixteenth-century tiles create an arched effect over the interior windows
of the Ramazan Efendi Mosque in Istanbul. Design is typical of Ottoman
tile art at its height. Courtesy of Kalebodur Seramik Sanayi A.S.

Photo by Nuri Bilge Ceylan

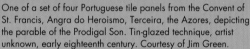

One of a set of four Portuguese tile panels from the Convent of St. Francis, Angra do Heroismo, Terceira, the Azores, depicting the parable of the Prodigal Son. Tin-glazed technique, artist unknown, early eighteenth century. Courtesy of Jim Green.

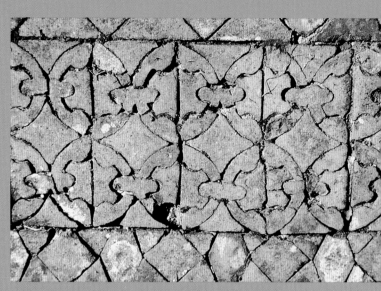

Clay tiles, dating from the twelfth century, cut in geometric shapes and arranged in patterns on the floor of the High Altar. Fountains Abbey, North Yorkshire, England.

shared their knowledge and skills with artisans from other cultures, tile techniques evolved and changed. The laborious mosaic work of early Persian craftsmen, who skillfully broke off standardized symbolic shapes from pieces of glazed tile and then created larger designs with them, gave way to a new technique, one which greatly simplified the mosaic process while maintaining a similar aesthetic effect. In this technique, later referred to as *cuerda seca*, a linear pattern was painted onto the surface of a tile with a substance designed to resist a glaze. When glazes were applied, the line of painted resist served as a barrier between the glaze colors.

Originally developed in Persia, the cuerda seca technique is also in evidence throughout the Alhambra—the fortress built by the Moors during the latter half of the fourteenth century—in Granada, Spain. A similar effect was obtained by separating glaze colors with raised ridges, which were formed by pressing the clay into molds.

During China's Tang Dynasty (A.D. 618-906), Chinese porcelains were introduced into Persia and the West, with far-reaching effects. Artisans endeavored for centuries thereafter to reproduce this exotic ware from local materials. The Persians, for example, developed a white tin glaze to mask their red clays; brightly colored designs could then be successfully applied to the clay's white surface.

Revived by eleventh-century Spanish tile makers, tin-glazed ware was called *maiolica* by the Italians, who acquired the technique via the island of Majorca in the Mediterranean. At the start of the sixteenth century, craftsmen in Holland also developed a version of this ware, which was later named *Delft* after one of the Dutch towns in which the tiles were made. The English soon produced tin-glazed ware, too; it was virtually identical in appearance to that of the Dutch. Many of

these blue-and-white tiles depicted the fashions, games, myths, and stories popular at the time; they continue to provide an important historic record.

During the twelfth century, Christian monasteries throughout western Europe and the British Isles provided the setting for the production of handcrafted tiles that had incised or raised designs. These tiles were made in a variety of shapes and sizes and were used to decorate the floors of churches and abbeys. Earthy and somewhat crude in appearance, they were either glazed in darker tones or left unglazed and were frequently arranged in geometric patterns not unlike the earlier Roman mosaic floors from which they were likely derived.

Inlaid tiles soon followed. In these, designs pressed into tiles were filled with contrasting clay colors. In England, inlaid tiles may be found in the Chapter House at Lichfield Cathedral and in the Retrochoir at Winchester Cathedral (both structures date from the thirteenth century), as well as in many parish churches. Unfortunately, the demise of the English monasteries during the early sixteenth-century reign of King Henry VIII resulted in the abandonment of inlaid tile production for the next three hundred years.

By the middle of the seventeenth century, tile making in Europe had become a full-fledged commercial enterprise, one spurred on by a growing population, international trade, and an evolving middle class. People had come to value sanitized surfaces, so tiles were used with greater frequency and imagination in the home. They were also exported from every country that made them, and artisans, who were now moving more freely about the Continent, adapted their skills to local materials and customs. The Dutch East India Company and other international traders transported tiles to the Colonies and to other parts of the world, frequently using

Two "art" tiles, circa 1880, designed for use on a fireplace mantel.
Chelsea Keramic Art Works, Chelsea, Massachusetts. Private collection.

the tiles as ballast on ships leaving Europe.

By the early nineteenth century, the Industrial Revolution had taken hold in much of western Europe and Great Britain. Herbert Minton (1793-1858), born into an English family of highly regarded ceramists, was champion of a movement during this period to bring back inlaid tiles for the restoration of medieval abbeys, churches, and cathedrals. Minton bought shares in two important patents, the first (in 1835) to manufacture inlaid tiles and the second (in 1840) to produce buttons from clay dust. Minton foresaw the means of mass-producing tiles with these two patented processes. Dubbed *encaustic* at the time, his new inlaid floor tiles became exceedingly popular throughout the Commonwealth and the United States.

When Europeans first arrived on the North American continent, no evidence of a tile-making tradition existed. In the northeast and along the eastern seaboard, especially in emerging metropolitan areas, many of the immigrants who built homes continued to look to England and to the Continent for the tiles they needed. As a result, tile-importing companies were established in all of the major coastal cities.

As was the custom across the Atlantic, where the fireplace was the focal point of any room, tiles were commonly used to decorate mantels and hearths. Beginning in the 1850s, Minton's multicolored encaustics were combined with geometric arrangements of unglazed tiles in various colors to cover the floors of domestic and commercial entryways. They were also used for the grand hallways of public buildings; the Senate wing of the United States Capitol provides an excellent example.

As the United States emerged from the Reconstruction period that followed the Civil War, people were once again able to focus their attention on domestic matters. Tiles soon became a virtual necessity in any fashionable home; they were seen as a reflection of the homeowner's good taste and social position. In spite of their increased status, however, most of the tiles used in the United States were still imported from overseas.

The Centennial Exposition of 1876, held in Philadelphia, signified a major turning point in American tile production. European manufacturers put on an impressive display of both pottery and tiles, and from that time on, American craftsmen and entrepreneurs embraced the challenge of tile making. Within a few years, manufactories, which frequently made use of European technology and personnel, had sprung up in Massachusetts, New York, New Jersey, Pennsylvania, Ohio, and Indiana.

The first decorative tiles in the United States were called *art* tiles, and they reflected the aesthetics and manufacturing methods prevalent in the British Isles and on the Continent. Produced primarily as ornamentation, art tiles were for the most part relief tiles and often depicted natural scenes or classical motifs. Made from clay dust, they were produced in bulky screw presses and were colored with glossy, translucent glazes applied over a white clay body. The machinery used to make these early tiles was rudimentary; a great deal of handwork was also involved. The presses were manually operated, and much of the finishing work and glazing was done by hand as well. Most notably, an original of each decorative tile had to be modeled in clay by an experienced artist-craftsman before the tile went into production.

Chelsea, Massachusetts, just north of Boston, was an early center of North American tile making. There, members of the Robertson family from Scotland gathered in the late 1860s and soon thereafter established the Chelsea Keramic Art Works. James, the father, was

The J. & J.G. Low Art Tile Works of Chelsea, Massachusetts, was known for its innovative tile designs. Any one of these would have been used as an accent on either corner of a fireplace opening. Circa 1880. Private collection.

a second-generation potter. Each of his three sons, Alexander, Hugh, and George, would eventually establish a pottery of his own, and each would add greatly to the ceramic tradition in the United States.

One apprentice at the Chelsea Keramic Art Works was John Gardner Low (1835-1907). After visiting the Exposition in Philadelphia, Low, with financial backing provided by his father, founded the J. & J. G. Low Art Tile Works, which produced award-winning tiles known for their innovative designs. Low's *natural process* tiles, for example, were made by pressing grasses, leaves, and other organic matter into the soft clay surface before firing. Low employed Arthur Osborne, an Englishman, as his chief modeler; Osborne designed many of the Low fireplace tiles as well as *plastic sketches*—large rectangular ceramic plaques that were used to decorate walls.

Isaac Broome (1835-1922), a French Canadian by birth, was one of the finest portrait tile modelers in the United States. An established artist and sculptor as well as a talented and prolific designer, Broome joined the Trent Tile Company of Trenton, New Jersey in 1883 and then assisted in the founding of the Providential Tile Works (also located in Trenton) in 1886. Four years later, he moved to western Pennsylvania to work at the Beaver Falls Art Tile Company. Unlike an employee today, whose work is owned by the company that employs him, Broome took full advantage of his diverse employment by modeling identical tiles for each of these companies.

Zanesville, Ohio, became a major site for tile manufacturing. In 1876, the Zanesville-located American Encaustic Tiling Company, which later grew to be the largest tile company in the world, started by producing unglazed geometric floor tiles at a price slightly less than the English equivalents. Over its nearly sixty years of operation, the company made virtually every type of tile imaginable.

In 1887, the company hired Herman Mueller (1854-1941), a German-born artist and sculptor, who expand-ed American Encaustic's product line to include art tiles of the highest quality. Within a short time, Mueller had devised a new method for producing encaustic tiles, and in 1894, together with chemist Karl Langenbeck, he left American Encaustic to form the Mosaic Tile Company (also located in Zanesville), a company which would soon become another giant of the industry. Both men became frustrated by the commercial orientation of Mosaic Tile. In 1903, Mueller left that company to found his own—the Mueller Mosaic Company—in Trenton, New Jersey.

The emergence, beginning in the late 1890s, of handcrafted, decorative tiles in the United States represented a rebellion against the conventional aesthetics of the Victorian era, a period during which tiles were viewed as mere ornaments—symbols of refined taste. The Victorian commercialization of both product and process as well as the impersonality of the work place left little room for free expression by the artist or craftsman. Although tiles had become less expensive and more widespread in use, most were mass-produced and lacked aesthetic appeal.

By the turn of the century, American appreciation of individual craftsmanship had developed significantly. This growth was inspired in part by the Arts and Crafts movement in England. There, in reaction to the deprivation brought on by the Industrial Revolution, artisans asserted their creativity through their crafts, rejuvenating the work place, and in theory, society as well. Individual tiles in America, previously manufactured as ornamental objects that would also serve a useful purpose once installed, became an artistic medium and a means of self-expression for the craftsman. Subject matter was simplified; glossy translucent glazes were replaced with matte finishes. The way a tile was produced had become an essential part of the way it looked; its handcrafted qualities were quite deliberately made visible.

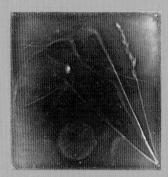

This pair of classical figures, designed for either side of a fireplace opening, may well have been modeled by Herman Mueller for the American Encaustic Tiling Company of Zanesville, Ohio, circa 1890. Private collection.

Christopher Columbus arriving on the North American shore. St. Nicholas Church, Zanesville, Ohio, 1898. This mural exemplifies Herman Mueller's new system for producing encaustic tiles at the Mosaic Tile Company in Zanesville.

Top: Tile designed by Arthur Osborne for the J. & J.G. Low Art Tile Works of Chelsea, Massachusetts, circa 1880. Note the mark in the lower right-hand corner, an encircled A. Private collection.

Second tile down: The "natural process" tiles were among the most unusual produced by the J. & J.G. Low Art Tile Works of Chelsea, Massachusetts, circa 1880. Private collection.

Two tiles immediately above: Portrait tiles designed for the two upper corners of a fireplace surround. Modeled by Isaac Broome for the Trent Tile Company, Trenton, New Jersey, circa 1885. Private collection.

One of over four hundred pictorial mosaic panels designed for the floor of the Pennsylvania State Capitol in Harrisburg, 1903. Henry Chapman Mercer, Moravian Pottery and Tile Works, Doylestown, Pennsylvania.

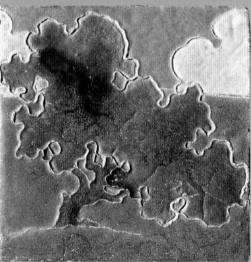

Top: *John Fitch's Boat*. Designed by Henry Chapman Mercer at the Moravian Pottery and Tile Works, Doylestown, Pennsylvania. Private collection. Courtesy of Vance Koehler.

Second tile down: Tile by Grueby Faience Company, Boston, Massachusetts, circa 1905. Private collection.

Rookwood faience produced by the Rookwood Pottery, Cincinnati, Ohio, 1915. Private residence, Columbus, Ohio.

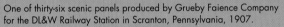

One of thirty-six scenic panels produced by Grueby Faience Company for the DL&W Railway Station in Scranton, Pennsylvania, 1907.

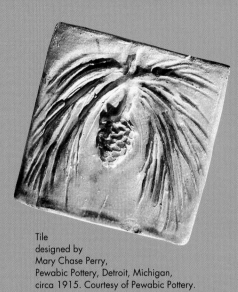

Tile
designed by
Mary Chase Perry,
Pewabic Pottery, Detroit, Michigan,
circa 1915. Courtesy of Pewabic Pottery.
Photo by B. Korab

Instrumental in bringing about these substantive changes was Henry Chapman Mercer (1856-1930), who redirected what had been a primarily functional focus on tiles to an artistic one. Mercer's influence stretched from coast to coast. Born into a wealthy family in Doylestown, Pennsylvania, he studied law at Harvard, and as a young man, traveled to Europe on a number of occasions. In 1898, he abandoned his active career as an archaeologist to take up tile making, working at first in small outbuildings in his own backyard. He named his enterprise—the Moravian Pottery and Tile Works—after the German-born stove plate makers who had settled nearby over a century earlier. In fact, some of Mercer's earliest tiles were taken from stove plate designs.

Very different from a manufacturing facility, Mercer's tile works was similar to an artisan's studio, where plaster molds were made from individually hand-modeled tiles. Multiple tiles were then produced by hand pressing soft clay into the molds. Mercer's simple and straightforward designs were often based on historic subjects dating back to medieval times. Although he produced tiles for domestic use, especially for fireplace surrounds, he was also involved in a number of large commercial projects. One of Mercer's early commissions (in 1903) entailed providing the floor tile for the State Capitol in Harrisburg, Pennsylvania. For that site, Mercer produced approximately four hundred mosaic murals, which depicted the history of the state, as decorative insets.

Several contemporaries of Mercer's also espoused Arts and Crafts's principles and were strongly influenced by the tile maker from Doylestown. Among the best known was William Grueby (1867-1925), a tile pioneer from Boston who apprenticed at the Low Art Tile Works for several years before branching out on his own. In 1894 he formed the Grueby Faience Company, and by the turn of the century, his matte green glaze

was emulated by many of the established potteries.

The simplicity of many of Grueby's designs, especially those that were custom made for particular installations, lent itself to a method known as *tube-line decoration*, a technique of which Grueby made frequent use. The outline of the design was formed by a ridge of clay that was applied by hand to the surface of the tile in order to separate contrasting glaze colors. In 1907, Grueby was commissioned to produce thirty-six panels for the interior of the new DL&W Railway Station in Scranton, Pennsylvania. These panels—each a masterpiece of American ceramic art—depicted specific scenes along the railroad.

In 1880, Maria Longworth Nichols founded the Rookwood Pottery, in Cincinnati, Ohio. This company started to produce tile and other architectural products in 1902. Rookwood tile, noted for its high relief and waxy matte glaze treatments, found its way into numerous prestigious installations, both in commercial buildings and in upscale private homes. Often entire stories, from floor to ceiling, would be covered with tiles, each tile having been custom made for the particular installation. Among the most spectacular examples were the Della Robbia Room in New York City's Vanderbilt Hotel, the Norse Room in Pittsburgh's Fort Pitt Hotel (both demolished), and the Rathskeller Room in the Seelbach Hotel in Louisville, Kentucky.

In 1896, Horace Caulkins, owner of a dental supply company in Detroit, engaged Mary Chase Perry (1867-1961) to promote his *Revelation Kiln* to the clay community. The kiln, which had already become popular among dentists, had obvious potential in the ceramics field, and Perry traveled throughout the northeastern states demonstrating its key features. The kiln was a commercial triumph and was not without rewards for Miss Perry. In 1903, together with Caulkins, she founded the Pewabic Pottery, which was named after the

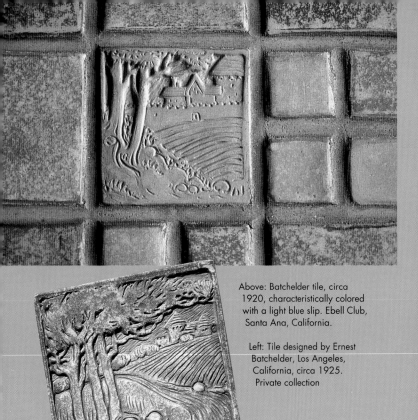

Above: Batchelder tile, circa 1920, characteristically colored with a light blue slip. Ebell Club, Santa Ana, California.

Left: Tile designed by Ernest Batchelder, Los Angeles, California, circa 1925. Private collection

Portion of a large tile mural produced at Claycraft Potteries, Los Angeles, California, 1929. Gadsden Hotel, Douglas, Arizona.

Pewabic Mine in Miss Perry's birthplace, Hancock, Michigan. From the company's inception, both pottery and tiles were produced at Pewabic. The tiles, akin to Mercer's in many ways, clearly and intentionally demonstrated the creativity of the artist. Perry became most well known for her glazes, specifically her iridescent blues and purples, and she was commissioned by some of the most respected architects of the time for commercial jobs both inside and outside of Detroit. Pewabic tiles are found in numerous schools, libraries, and museums, as well as in many churches, including the National Shrine of the Immaculate Conception (in Washington, DC), which was tiled between 1924 and 1931.

The popularity of machine-made art tiles had diminished by the turn of the century and had all but disappeared by 1910. By this time, hand-crafted tiles—or those made by machine to appear handmade—dominated the market. Throughout the 1910s and 1920s, tiles were used with increasing imagination to decorate the walls and floors of various rooms in the home, as well as patios, walkways, and gardens. Tiles in contrasting colors and in varying shapes and sizes were used in the same installation, often with striking results. In more expensive homes, decorative liners and mural work became more commonplace. Bright colors and geometric patterns were particularly popular throughout the southern and western states. By the mid-1920s, ceramic tiles in many areas were more than a symbol of good taste; they had become an integral part of most new homes.

California lagged behind the rest of the country in the production of decorative tiles primarily because

eastern manufactories produced adequate quantities to meet California's demand. After the turn of the century, however, the state's population began to mushroom in major urban areas. Although some tiles were made in California as early as 1900, it was ten years later before a unique tile-making tradition was established there.

In 1901, Ernest Batchelder (1875-1957), born and educated in the East, came to California to teach design at Throop Polytechnic Institute in Pasadena. After two enlightening trips to Europe, he abandoned his successful teaching career in 1910 and started to make tiles in his backyard. The likely source of Batchelder's inspiration is evident in the tiles he chose for his own home. Embedded in the chimney outside, on the front door, and on the fireplace mantel—adjacent to Batchelder's own tiles—are Moravian tiles made by Henry Chapman Mercer.

Characteristically, Batchelder tiles were hand pressed from plaster molds and colored with clay slips rather than with glazes. By partially rubbing off the colorant to expose the clay underneath (thus leaving a mottled effect on the surface), Batchelder incorporated the clay body into the overall aesthetic of the tile. Both the material he used and his process of production became an integral part of his tiles' aesthetic. Like Mercer, Batchelder was drawn to medieval imagery, yet many of his tiles also include features of the California landscape.

By 1912 Batchelder had outgrown his backyard and had established a small factory in Pasadena. Eight years later, he moved again, this time to a much larger

Pair of handcrafted fireplace tiles designed by
Rufus Keeler, California Clay Products Company,
South Gate, California, 1925.

Brightly colored geometric designs produced
by California China Products Company,
National City, California, 1914. Santa Fe
Railroad depot, San Diego, California.

Tile mural produced at the
Malibu Potteries, Malibu,
California, 1929.
Adamson House, Malibu.

facility just north of downtown Los Angeles. There, at the
height of his production in the mid-1920s, he employed
up to 175 people. Batchelder exhibited his tiles in most
of the major cities in the United States. In addition to
many residential fireplace mantels, three of his largest
commissions, all extant, were the Chapel of Our Lady
of Victory at Saint Catherine's College in St. Paul,
Minnesota; the lobby of the Fine Arts Building in
downtown Los Angeles; and the lobby of the Marine
Building in Vancouver, British Columbia.

The earthy, handcrafted appearance of Batchelder's
tiles had a broad appeal, and the type of low-relief
design that he used attracted the attention of a handful
of other talented ceramists and businessmen who
wished to capitalize on his success. Among these
was Fred Robertson (1869-1952)—the grandson of the
founder of the Chelsea Keramic Art Works two generations earlier—who in 1921 became the superintendent
at Claycraft Potteries in Los Angeles.

The manufacturing process and overall aesthetic of
Claycraft tiles were similar to Batchelder's, but a unique
feature of Claycraft tiles was their depiction of specific
scenes along the California coast and the sublime land-
scapes of Yosemite National Park. Designed primarily
as inserts for fireplace mantels, other Claycraft tiles featured romanticized views of the California missions and
quaint settings from the early days of Spanish occupa-
tion. The detail and subtle coloration involved in each
design were truly remarkable.

Back in 1911, when Batchelder was grappling with
clay in his Pasadena backyard, a tile company of pro-

found importance was getting underway in National
City, just south of San Diego. California China Products
Company was founded by Walter Nordhoff (1858-1937),
a journalist-rancher turned entrepreneur who was com-
missioned to provide the tile for both the new Santa Fe
Railroad depot in San Diego and for the California
Building at Balboa Park, site of the Panama-California
International Exposition in 1915. The California
Building's brightly colored and geometrically patterned
tiles, extraordinary in their brilliance and craftsmanship,
were a perfect complement to the structure's Spanish
Colonial architecture and reflected the romanticized tra-
ditions of both Mexico and Spain. Had these tiles been
produced only for the Exposition, they could easily have
been dismissed as an aberration. But the tile aesthetic
that started in National City became extremely popular
throughout California and dominated both architecture
and interior design for the next twenty years.

Rufus B. Keeler (1885-1934) was another major player
in the manufacturing of decorative tiles in southern
California. In 1917, after working for a number of clay
products companies in the state, Keeler started his own
business handcrafting tiles for fireplace surrounds. With
help from local investors, he greatly expanded his operation in 1923, forming the California Clay Products
Company, (known as Calco), which produced both
brightly colored geometric tiles and a glazed version of
a press-molded tile that was more in the style of Ernest
Batchelder. In 1926, Keeler was hired by May K. Rindge,
a wealthy widow in Malibu, to build a tile pottery (Malibu
Potteries) there on the beach. For the next six years,

Tiles were commonly used to decorate stair risers. Solon & Schemmel, San Jose, California, circa 1928.

Tiles by California Faience, Berkeley, California, circa 1926. Hearst Castle, San Simeon, California.

under Keeler's management, the company produced some of the most beautiful tiles made in America. Malibu tiles can be found both in the Adamson House in Malibu, which was designated a Point of Historic Interest in 1985, and inside the Los Angeles City Hall, for which Malibu produced twenty-three large, decorative wall panels.

Among the handful of northern California companies producing handcrafted tiles during this time were Solon & Schemmel and California Faience. The former was founded in 1920 by Albert Solon (1887-1949) and Frank Schemmel (c. 1880-1950) in San Jose. Schemmel came from a prominent local family. Solon, an Englishman, could trace his tile-making roots back to the early seventeenth century; his ancestors in southern France had started a ceramics factory in the Pyrenees. The latter, California Faience, was founded in Berkeley five years earlier by William Bragdon (1884-1959) and Chauncey Thomas (1877-1950), both accomplished ceramists from the East. The most prestigious of their many tile installations was the palatial mansion of William Randolph Hearst at San Simeon, designed by architect Julia Morgan and built during the 1920s. Tiles are everywhere, both inside and out. Wall surfaces, floors, patio inserts, stair risers, friezes, chimney tops, and towers all create a striking display of pattern and color, one that enlivens the whole environment.

The Great Depression of the 1930s all but eliminated the tile industry in the United States, and the factories that survived were soon converted to support the war effort, which lasted well into the 1940s. After the war, tiles were in short supply, and factories were reestablished to meet the unprecedented postwar demand. But times had changed; the flare of the 1920s and early 1930s had expired. Tiles were once again mass-produced, this time in muted pastel colors and in standard sizes, with only minimal evidence of an interest in design. Handcrafted tiles had all but disappeared.

Following a lapse of nearly thirty years, the handcrafted tradition in tile making resurfaced during the 1960s, seemingly as an adjunct to contemporary pottery. A renewed focus on glaze treatments, surface textures, earth tones, and the overall aesthetic of the tile were its primary characteristics. Tiles were promoted as architectural products and were used to clad the exteriors of public buildings as well as the interiors of custom homes.

As the decade of the 1970s progressed and as the focus shifted from earth tones toward lighter, more neutral glazes, color became a more dominant concern. By the early 1980s, a preference for larger sizes and a cleaner, more pristine installation had evolved; inexpensive imported tiles, which met these demands, became particularly popular. Gradually, however, a renewed appreciation of individual craftsmanship became evident, and increasing numbers of handcrafted tiles reappeared.

By 1990 a substantial market for high-end, handcrafted ware had been established. Most major cities boasted dealers who specialized exclusively in these handmade tiles, and tiles were being promoted in the most imaginative of ways. No longer were they reserved for walls, floors, and kitchen or bathroom counters. Tile had become a decorative art form in and of itself; its use was limited only by the imagination.

The handcrafted tradition in tile-making, which dates back to prehistoric man's first recognition of clay as a medium for artistic expression, is at present experiencing a renaissance the likes of which has never been seen in the United States. Literally hundreds of tile artists, tile artisans, muralists, and mosaicists have emerged from their backyards and small studios across the country, and many of the larger manufacturers have refocused their production to include decorative lines. Today, there is no question that tile history is being made.

CHAPTER TWO

GETTING STARTED

Lynda Curtis
Condah. 1992
14" x 10"
(35.6 x 25.4 cm)
Photograph by
Van Blerck Photography

Frank Giorgini
Sea Turtles. 1991
6" x 6" (15.2 x 15.2 cm)
Photograph by Bobby Hansson

Elizabeth Grajales
Untitled. 1993
7-1/2" x 8-1/2" (19.1 x 21.6 cm)

Kilns

The *kiln* is the heating chamber in which clay is *fired* (or heated) to irreversible hardness and is the most important piece of equipment in the tile-making process. A kitchen oven can't do a kiln's job; its temperatures aren't high enough to cause the chemical reaction that turns clay into a hard material. Once you understand the kiln's function and purpose, you will find it much easier to make and decorate your tiles.

Usually, clay tiles are fired twice in the kiln, first in what's known as a *bisque* (or biscuit) *firing* and then in a *glaze firing*. The bisque firing both hardens the tile and makes it easier to handle (dry, unfired clay is brittle and fragile). The glaze firing melts the glaze that's on your tile into a protective, glasslike coating. (For more information on firing your tiles, see chapters 8 and 10.)

Kilns differ in several respects. A kiln's size, its firing range, and the fuel that it uses—electricity, gas, or a solid fuel such as wood—may affect the type of tile that you make and the ways in which you decorate it.

An electric kiln, for example, will limit you to what's known as *oxidation firing*—the simple application of heat. A gas-fueled kiln, on the other hand, offers *reduction firing*, in which the ratio of air to gas is adjusted at certain stages to give a fuel-rich and oxidation-starved atmosphere. This atmosphere brings out specific colors in clays and often results in spectacular and unique stoneware glaze colors that *break* (or disperse) over the surface of the clay. (The bluish orange glaze on my *Turtles* tile—shown above—is an excellent example.) With creativity and practice, however, you should be able to achieve equally satisfying results with an electric kiln.

Firing ranges (the temperatures to which a given kiln is capable of firing) also vary from kiln to kiln. A small, electric test kiln that runs on household current may have a lower firing range than a large commercial kiln; the test kiln may not provide the high temperatures required to

fire some clays and glazes. This limitation, however, won't be of much concern to the beginning tile maker.

The temperature within a kiln is monitored by means of *pyrometric cones*. These are small, pyramid- or bar-shaped pieces of clay that are manufactured to melt at specific, designated temperatures. When you fire the kiln, you'll usually make up what's known as a *cone pack* (Photo 1) and position it inside the kiln. This is a wad of moist clay into which are placed one or more cones. When the kiln is fired, the cones melt, one at a time, as the kiln temperatures rise. By watching the cone pack through a peephole in the kiln, you'll be able to gauge the kiln temperatures visually.

1

Almost all electric kilns can be purchased with a *cone sitter*. This is a small mechanism that functions in conjunction with a pyrometric cone to turn the kiln off when the interior temperatures reach a specific point. A bar-shaped or small regular cone is inserted into the sitter, where it rests on two prongs. A lever rests on top of the cone. As long as the cone remains solid, it prevents the lever from moving downward, but when the cone slumps, one end of the lever lowers, the other end rises,

Suzanne DeMott Gaadt
Celtic Knots. 1992
4" x 4" (10.2 x 10.2 cm)

George Handy
Untitled. 1993
8" x 8" (20.3 x 20.3 cm)

and a hook at that end releases a latch which flaps down, smacks a button, and shuts off the kiln.

Cone packs should always be used as a safety precaution, even when the kiln has an automatic sitter. *Pyrometric gauges* are also available; these read the kiln temperatures electronically. Cones, however, are more accurate. Electric kilns should also be equipped with a timer with a safety override.

In order to use the kiln's interior space efficiently, you'll arrange your tiles on *kiln furniture*—shelves and holders made from a ceramic material that won't melt during the firing. Kiln furniture accessories are available to accommodate tiles. In the upper left-hand corner of Photo 2 is a block-shaped tile-setter unit with small shelves for individual tiles; to its right is a stacking unit; and shown in the foreground are two types of corner holders.

2

If you don't have a kiln of your own, the best way to gain access to firing facilities is by taking a ceramics course at your local college or university. You'll also find expert help there when you need it. Classes at hobby ceramics centers are another possibility. Generally, these centers specialize in the application of commercial *underglazes* (which, as their name suggests, go under glazes) to *greenware* (clay that has not yet been bisque fired), but the center may be able to arrange firing for your handmade tiles. Your clay supply outlet may also have firing facilities.

If you don't have access to any firing facilities, consider purchasing a small, electric test kiln. Many of these operate on household current and are reasonably inexpensive. Though their interiors may provide less than one cubic foot (.028 cubic meter) of space, in combination with the appropriate tile setters, they are capable of firing ten or so 4" x 4" (10.2 cm x 10.2 cm) tiles at a time. And when you're first getting started, you'll gain more experience by firing a small kiln often than a big kiln less frequently. Firing a test kiln will let you experiment—and learn—faster. Even after you've become a pro, you'll use your test kiln often to obtain quick results on small samples of clay or glazes.

If you do purchase a kiln, be sure to refer to the manufacturer's instructions before you fire it for the first time; kilns vary greatly in their methods of operation. You should also be extremely careful to set it up properly. Don't place a kiln in your living space; the chemicals given off during firing can be toxic. Instead, place the kiln in a separate room or outbuilding and make sure that it's properly positioned and well ventilated (see chapter 16). A small electric test kiln should be placed at least three feet (91.4 cm) away from combustible materials and at least one foot (30.5 cm) above the floor. Protect the floor with an asbestos-substitute, fireproof covering.

Clay

The clay that you'll be using to make the tiles described in this book is a composite of natural, earthen materials that turns hard when it is fired. It's usually sold in 25-pound (11.4 kg) plastic bags, is moist, pliable, and

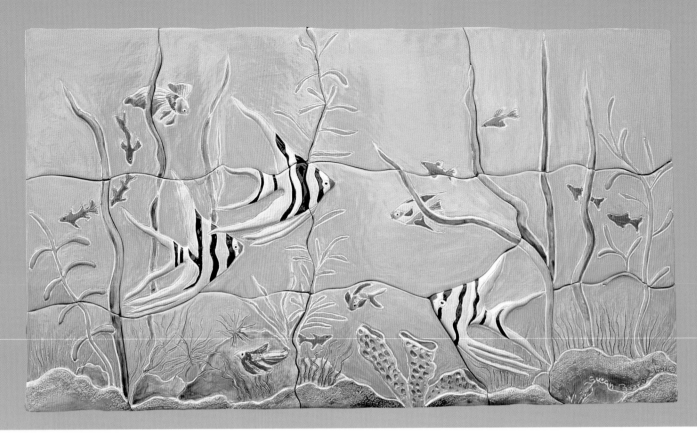

ready-to-use, and can be purchased from ceramics supply distributors or from some craft outlets. If it's kept in its moist state, this clay will last indefinitely and will actually improve with age. When it dries out, it can be processed back to its plastic state by crumbling the dry pieces and adding water. (For reasons of health, you should be careful when you do this; see chapter 16 for details.)

Many types of clay are available, each with its own properties and firing characteristics. Your choice of which type to use will be influenced by several factors, among them the type and purpose of the object you're making and the hardness that results from the particular clay's firing range. Color and texture are also considerations. A basic understanding of clay types and clay firing will help you to select wisely.

The chemical definition of clay is hydrated silicate of aluminum. *Primary* (or *residual*) *clays* are pure clays and are closest to this definition. Like all clays, primary clays are formed through the geological weathering of igneous rocks, but unlike other types of clay, they don't travel far from their source. China clay, from which porcelain is made, is a primary clay; it typically fires to whiteness.

Most other clays are classified as *secondary clays*. After decomposing from the parent rock, these clays are transported by water and ice to a new location, picking up impurities such as minerals and organic matter along the way and usually ending up as a sedimentary deposit at the mouth of a river or at the bottom of an ocean.

Though not as chemically pure as primary clays, secondary clays are more plastic. In addition, their impurities cause them to fire to many different colors in an earthen range of grays, tans, browns, and reds. Iron oxide is the most common impurity that results in these variations of color. The reddish color of terra cotta, a secondary clay, results from its iron oxide content.

In selecting a clay, your primary consideration will be the *clay body* (the nature and proportions of its ingredients). For tile work, your best choice will probably be what's known as a *sculpture body*, which has a fair amount of *grog* (prefired and pulverized clay) in it. A clay that's identified as a *throwing clay* won't be as good a choice because it will contain little or no grog. The grog, which makes the clay slightly gritty to the touch, will give your tile strength and will help to keep it from warping. High-fire porcelain, which has a low grog content, will yield beautiful whites and will provide a good base for bright glaze colors, but porcelain is prone to warping when used in the format of a flat tile.

You will also need to consider the clay's *cone-firing range*, the upper range of temperatures to which a given type of clay can be fired. This range is often indicated by the symbol Δ and is established according to an industry-standardized temperature-rating system. A stoneware Δ 10 clay, for example, can be fired up to 2300°F (1260°C).

Appendix A on page 137 provides temperature equivalents for each cone-firing range. Notice in this chart that the cone-firing numbers run from cone 022, a very low temperature range, up to cone 10, a very high range.

When a clay is fired to the upper end of its firing range, it reaches *maturity*, the stage at which its molecular structure becomes extremely dense and the clay becomes nonporous, waterproof, and glasslike. The firing range, and therefore the maturity point, of a given clay will vary depending upon the clay's composition. *Earthenware clays* such as terra cotta, for example, which are low-firing (usually below 2000°F or 1093°C)

Opposite page: Susan Beere
Aquarium. 1991
18" x 32" (45.7 x 81.3 cm)
Photograph by Hugh L. Wilkerson

Above left: Heather Blume
Bonfire Tile. 1992
4" x 4" (10.2 x 10.2 cm)
Photograph by Heather Blume

Above right: Nawal and Karim Motawi
Celtic Knot. 1992
8" x 8" (20.3 x 20.3 cm)
Photograph by Nawal Motawi

Right: Bettina Elsner
Terra Cotta "Carpet." 1989
48" x 36" (121.9 x 91.4 cm)

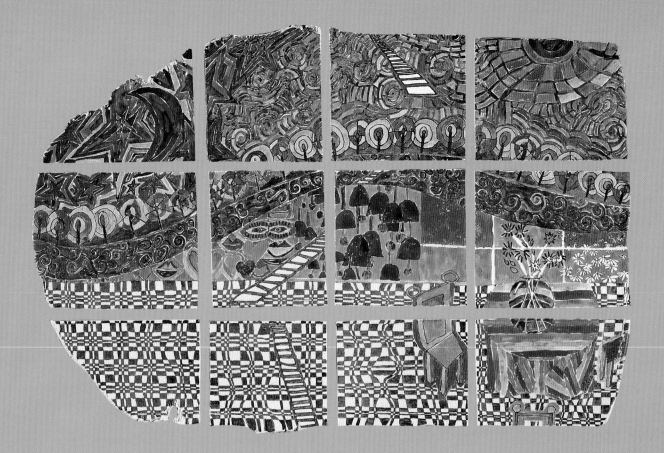

Above: Barbara Schwartz
Night Turns into Day—
Life of the Artist. 1990
18" x 28" (45.7 x 71.1)

Left: Carrie Anne Parks
Vines. 1991
28" x 21" x 4-1/2"
(71.1 x 53.3 x 11.4 cm)

Joseph A. Triplo
Dining Room Table. 1991
Without leaves: 40" x 71"
(101.6 x 180.3 cm)
Photograph by Dave Palmer

and porous, will mature at much lower temperatures than *stoneware clays*—hard and dense clays that fire above 2000°F (1093°C).

A clay's maximum firing temperature is known as its point of *vitrification*. When the clay is fired at temperatures any higher, it will deform and eventually melt down to become a hardened puddle on the kiln shelf. (Note that kiln furniture, described earlier, is made from a material that won't reach its vitrification point before your tiles do. Kiln furniture is rated for high or low firing. If you're going to be firing in the stoneware range, be sure that your kiln furniture is rated for high temperatures.)

Firing temperatures may also affect the clay's color. Terra cotta will fire to many different shades of redness. When it's fired to cone 06, it turns rosy red, but when the clay is fired to its maturity point—around cone 2—its color deepens to brown.

The glazes with which you'll cover your tiles also have firing ranges. A cone 06 to cone 04 glaze, for example, is a standard low-fire glaze. For more complete descriptions of glazes and underglazes, see chapters 7 and 9.

The way in which you intend to use your tiles should also be considered. Your tile may not need to be fired to maturity in order to be functional. If you were making a tile for a living-room wall, firing the clay to a nonporous, waterproof state would not be necessary. You might select a stoneware clay, which could be successfully fired to sufficient hardness at lower temperature ranges than those required for vitrification. A clay with a low-fire temperature range—a standard bisque-firing range of cone 06 to cone 04—would be adequate. If you were making floor tiles, on the other hand, you would probably choose a low stoneware clay, with a cone 2 range up to high-fire stoneware cone 10, for strength.

For exterior installations in wet areas, your tiles must be brought to the vitrification point or very close to it. Even with a glaze over its surface, a tile fired at a lower range can absorb moisture through its unglazed back surface, and this moisture will discolor the glaze or cause it to flake off. If you selected a stoneware cone 10 clay and bisque-fired your tile up to cone 2, painted a low-fire glaze cone 06 onto it, and then fired it to cone 06, the resulting tile would be strong enough for indoor use on a floor or wall, but the clay body itself would still be somewhat porous because the clay was never fired to its point of vitrification—cone 10. You wouldn't want to use this tile in a continually wet area such as a shower wall.

A lower-firing terra cotta, on the other hand, could work very well in an outdoor environment. Though the vitrification point of this clay might be as low as cone 2, if you fire the clay to that point, it will become nonporous.

You'll usually be able to get help selecting a clay at a ceramics supply store, and the recommendations offered by the people there will be especially important if you don't have a kiln and plan to use their firing facilities.

Tools and Equipment

As well as a kiln or access to one, you will need some basic pottery tools (shown on the lower left-hand corner of the canvas in Photo 3 on page 26). Though these items can be bought separately, your local ceramics store or craft store is likely to carry a packaged set, including a *pin tool* (also referred to as a *potter's pin* or *pin*), a *trimming tool*, a wooden *sculpting tool*, a wood *rib*, a *cut-off wire*, and a sponge. To make your first flat clay tiles, you should also have the items in the list that follows.

Two strips of wood, 3/8" or 1/2" (1.0 cm or 1.3 cm) thick
Pieces of canvas

Libby Donohoe
Siena Deer. 1992
4" x 15-1/4" (10.2 x 38.7 cm)

Sections of smooth board or wallboard,
    about 16" x 20" (40.6 cm x 50.8 cm)
Rolling pin
Metric ruler
Straightedge
90° angle or square
Pencil
Cardboard, mat board, or Masonite
Sheets of clear plastic or plastic bags

As you begin to experiment with different tile-making and glazing techniques, you'll also want to

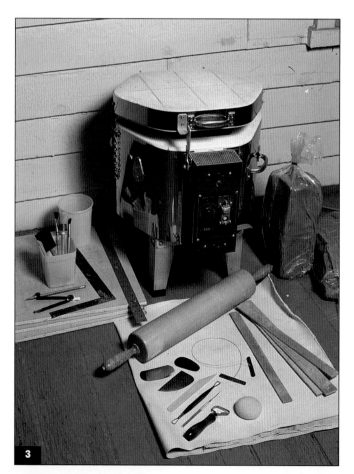

have other tools and supplies on hand. Each of these is described in subsequent chapters, and with the help of the information in chapter 14, you'll be able to make many of these items yourself. Others are technique-specific, so wait until you decide which techniques to try before you spend your hard-earned money.

Work Space

For beginners, who will be working on a small scale, a complete studio won't be necessary, but if you don't have access to a classroom or commercial studio, you'll need to set up a space of your own—one that isn't a part of your living space. Clay dust and glaze materials must be kept out of your home. An outbuilding is ideal; a garage or a basement with good ventilation and a separate entrance can be used in a pinch.

Your studio should have a flat working surface and running water, and it must be well ventilated. Once you start making large quantities of tiles from moist clay, it will also need to be large enough to accommodate shelves or *drying racks* (similar to baking racks) to hold boards stacked with drying tiles, as well as accumulated glaze supplies and additional tools.

Making use of a college or professional ceramic studio can be an economical and space-saving alternative to gradually taking over your own property. If your budget is tight and you don't have a vacant outbuilding, enroll in a ceramics course!

Important safety guidelines are provided in chapter 16; read them carefully. And as you set up your studio and work in it, keep three basic rules in mind: Work "wet," clean "wet," and clean compulsively! Your goal is to avoid creating clay dust. When you can't avoid it, remove it without stirring it up. Wipe your tools and all horizontal surfaces down frequently with a damp sponge, and plan on ways to keep from tracking any dust into your home. Make sure that your space is well ventilated. Wear surgical or plastic gloves and an appropriate OSHA-approved mask that will filter mist and dust when you're using glaze chemicals. Whether the glazes are in powdered or liquid form, many of the colorants in them are composed of toxic metallic oxides.

CHAPTER THREE

MAKING A FLAT TILE

Tamara Jaeger
Moroccan Stars. 1991
6" x 6" (15.2 x 15.2 cm)
Photograph by Chas Krider

Natalie Surving
Sea Turtle. 1991
4" x 4" (10.2 x 10.2 cm)

Frank Giorgini
Afro Tile. 1992
12" x 12" (30.5 x 30.5 cm)
Photograph by Bobby Hansson

Making a Slab

To make tile shapes, you'll first need to cut a chunk of moist clay from your large bag and roll it out into a slab. Start by spreading out a piece of canvas or stretching it over a flat board. Peel back the plastic from the bag, and using your cut-off wire, slice off a 2"- to 3"-thick (5.1 cm to 7.6 cm) chunk of clay (Photo 4). Place the chunk on the canvas-covered board. Make a habit of removing the moist clay that's left on the wire by running two fingers along the wire (Photo 5) and pushing the clay that you collect back into the bag or into your work. If you don't, these bits of clay may dry out, fall off the wire, and crumble into clay dust—something to be avoided.

Then, using the heel of your hand, pound the slab into a roughly flat shape. If you like, you can help flatten and stretch out the slab by picking it up and tossing it at an angle against the canvas-covered board. Next, select two strips of wood, both 3/8" or 1/2" (1.0 cm or 1.3 cm) thick, and place one on each side of the slab. The sticks should be parallel to each other and spaced no farther apart than the length of your rolling pin (Photo 6).

Lay another piece of canvas on top of the slab and

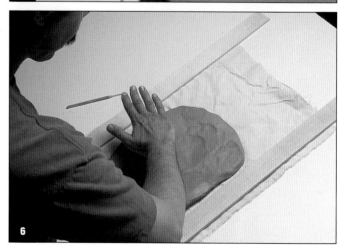

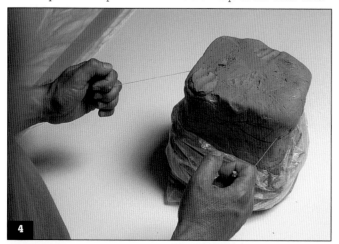

strips. Rest the rolling pin on top of the covered strips (Photo 7) and start rolling. The canvas will keep the rolling pin from sticking, and the strips will ensure that the entire slab is rolled to a uniform thickness. Remember, if this method is to be effective, the rolling pin should be moved back and forth across the strips until it rides evenly along their full length (Photo 8).

Kathy Triplett
City Hall (from Pack
Place series). 1992
Each 8" x 8"
(20.3 x 20.3 cm)
Photograph by Kathy Triplett

When you're making a large number of tiles, a *slab roller* (Photo 9) comes in handy, but beginners certainly don't need to purchase this piece of equipment. The slab roller produces slabs of uniform thickness by forcing clay between two horizontal cylinders or under one cylinder. It's a large piece of equipment and will require a large portion of your work space, but it will also serve

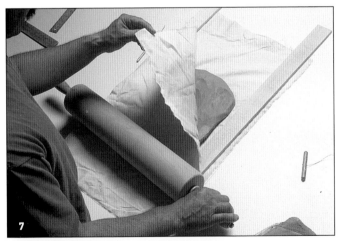

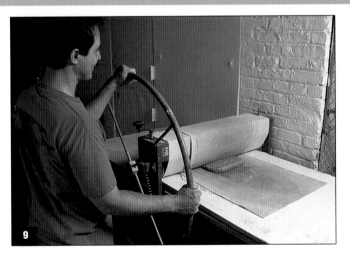

as a very effective work table when it's not being used for slab production. Slab rollers come with manufacturer's directions for use; read them carefully.

Transferring the Slab

In order to measure, cut, and dry your tiles, you'll need to transfer the slab to another flat surface. If you cut your tiles to shape on the canvas and then have to transfer them from it, you will run the risk of deforming them. Moving the slab now will also free up your worktable for rolling out more slabs.

There are several ways to transfer the slab. If you've rolled it out on a canvas-covered wooden board or piece of wallboard, place a piece of wallboard on top of the slab. (A wooden board can be used for this purpose, but the moisture that it absorbs from the slab will cause it to warp. Covering this wooden board with canvas or with several layers of newspaper will help to prevent moisture absorption.) Then flip over the sandwiched slab. The slab will now rest upside down on the wallboard.

If you've rolled a texture into the surface of the slab (see page 59) and want that original, textured side to

Cairo Cocalis
Psycho Kitty. 1992
6" x 6" (15.2 x 15.2 cm)
Photograph by Elizabeth Vanderkooy

Frank D'Amico
Untitled. 1993
14" x 12" (35.6 x 30.5 cm)
Photograph by Frank D'Amico

face up, just repeat the procedure with another piece of wallboard. (Note that pieces of wallboard or wooden boards should be discarded as soon as they begin to retain clay or the clay no longer separates cleanly from them. The clay dust that old boards are likely to trap can be hazardous to your health.)

If your slab rests on canvas only and isn't supported by a board, proceed as follows. After placing a piece of wallboard on top of the slab, lift one end of the canvas, holding it tightly against that end of the board. As you flip the slab over, it will flex with the canvas; bend and stretch it as little as possible. Though clay should relax flat, it sometimes has a "memory," and even if you flatten the deformed slab again, it will be more prone to warping during the later drying and firing stages.

Attempting to lift the slab with your fingers may cause it to stretch, deform, or even rip. If you don't have wallboard or wooden boards on hand, place flat sticks

above and below the slab (two rulers will work) and hold the slab gently between them as you lift (Photo 10). By spreading out the pressure needed to hold the slab, you'll minimize distortion of the clay.

Calculating Shrinkage

Because clay shrinks as it dries and again as it is fired, your original tile must be larger than the size that you want your finished tile to be. Every clay has a different *percentage of shrinkage;* each will shrink a different amount depending upon the temperature to which you fire it. For these reasons, you'll need to calculate the shrinkage of the particular clay that you're using.

Catalogue descriptions of purchased clay will usually indicate the percentage of shrinkage at a designated firing temperature. In general, the higher the temperature to which the clay is fired, the greater the shrinkage. Clays with more grog or *filler* (sawdust, straw, or sand, for example) usually shrink less than others.

The most accurate way to determine shrinkage at a particular temperature is to make clay *test strips* and fire them. Roll out a small slab of the clay from which your tiles will be made and cut it into several strips, each about 1-1/2" (3.8 cm) wide, 6" (15.2 cm) long, and 3/8" to 1/2" (1.0 cm to 1.3 cm) thick. (See the next section, "Cutting Tile Shapes," for instructions on the cutting process.) With a metric ruler, measure and mark each strip at 10 cm, as shown in Photo 11. Metric measurements will make calculating percentages much easier.

Before you test fire each of these strips at a different temperature, use your pin to mark the soft clay with the cone number to which you'll be firing that strip. You may also want to note the type of clay body from which the strip was made (cone 10 stoneware or cone 6 sculpture

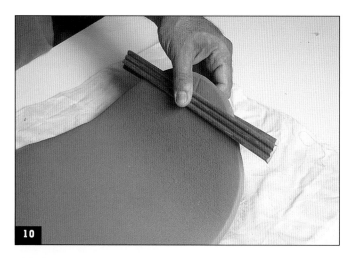

10

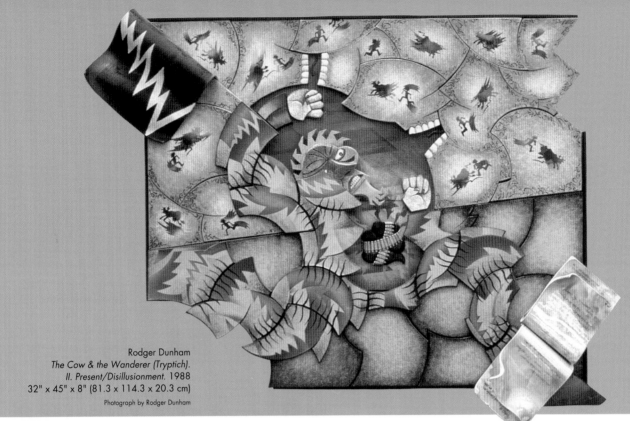

Rodger Dunham
The Cow & the Wanderer (Tryptich).
II. Present/Disillusionment. 1988
32" x 45" x 8" (81.3 x 114.3 x 20.3 cm)
Photograph by Rodger Dunham

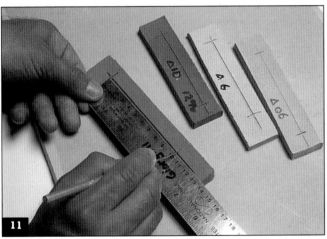

11

body, for example). Marking the strips will enable you to keep track of the results of your test firing.

After each of the test tiles has been fired (for firing instructions, see chapter 8), measure its length again. Then calculate the percentage of shrinkage. If the 10 cm mark is now 8.8 cm long, you have 12% shrinkage (100 mm - 88 mm = 12 mm; 12 mm = 12%).

The next step is to calculate how large to cut your tile in order to end up with a finished tile of the size that you want. The example that follows includes the formula that you'll use.

Finished tile size: 4" x 4" (10.2 cm x 10.2 cm)
Shrinkage: 12% at desired temperature range

M = Original moist clay tile size
S = Percentage of shrinkage
F = Finished tile size

Use the formula $(1 - S)M = F$

$$(1 - 12\%)M = 4$$
$$(0.88)M = 4$$
$$M = 4 \div 0.88$$
$$M = 4.54" (11.5 \text{ cm})$$

As you can see in this example, a 4-1/2" x 4-1/2" (11.4 cm x 11.4 cm) original moist clay tile will result in a tile very close to 4" x 4" (10.2 cm x 10.2 cm).

With this formula, as long as you know two of the variables, the third can always be calculated. To determine the percentage of shrinkage for an original moist clay tile that is 4-1/2" x 4-1/2" (11.4 cm x 11.4 cm), for instance, and a finished tile size of 4" x 4" (10.2 cm x 10.2 cm), just use the formula as follows:

$$(1 - S)M = F$$
$$(1 - S)4.5 = 4$$
$$1 - S = 4 \div 4.5$$
$$1 - S = 0.88$$
$$1 = 0.88 + S$$
$$1 - 0.88 = S$$
$$0.12 = S$$

The percentage of shrinkage is 12%.

Cutting Tile Shapes

To cut standard square or rectangular tiles from your rolled slab, you'll need a straightedge, a ruler, a large 90° angle or square, and a pin tool. Unlike a knife, the pin (with which you'll scribe the slab and cut the tiles) won't veer off course if your hand twists while you're using it. A knife tends to cut toward the angle at which the blade's surface is twisted; a pin, on the other hand, has no directional preference.

Before cutting your square or rectangular tiles, first visualize how to get as many as possible from the oval

Kathy Triplett
Crab (right) and *Deco Crab* (left). 1993
Each 6" x 6" (15.2 x 15.2 cm)
Photograph by Kathy Triplett

slab. Next, to make a grid on the slab, use your pin and straightedge to measure and scribe parallel lines every 4-1/2" (11.4 cm) or the desired length of a moist tile. Do this until you run out of space. Now use the angle or square to scribe perpendicular lines every 4-1/2" (11.4 cm) or the desired width of a moist tile. Check your measurements, and then, using the straightedge and pin tool, cut all the way through the scribed lines (Photo 12). Peel away the excess slab, wedge it up while it's still soft, and place it in a plastic bag for re-use.

To make patterns for geometric tile shapes, draw the shape on a large sheet of graph paper. Then place the paper pattern on top of the clay and transfer its lines by making a series of pin pricks through the pattern lines on the paper or by running a rounded pencil point along them. (Photo 16 on page 38 shows the pin-prick technique.) Remove the graph paper when you're finished and use your pin tool to cut all the way through the slab at the marked lines. The same method can be used to transfer nongeometric designs; just use ordinary paper instead.

Another accurate method for cutting flat tile shapes is to cut a *template* (or pattern) from a piece of cardboard, mat board, or thin Masonite. Then, for each tile that you plan to cut, use your pin to trace the template's outline onto the rolled slab. It's also possible to fabricate cookie-cutter type tools for cutting shapes; see

chapter 14 if you'd like to make your own. These tools are often equipped with a plunger that releases the tile from the tool.

When you want to repeat an intricate pattern of individual tiles—ones that aren't necessarily square—making a plaster mold of one section of the pattern can be helpful. By pressing the mold onto the slab, you will imprint outlines of the tile shapes that lie within that area of the pattern. (Instructions for making plaster molds are given in chapters 4, 5, and 6.)

For a unique and free-form effect, you can try cutting your tiles directly from the block of moist clay, as shown in Photo 13. By wiggling the cut-off wire as you slice off each slab, you will create a texture in the clay surface. If you'd like to try this technique, first pound the bag of clay into a shape that's roughly 4-1/2" x 4-1/2" (11.4 cm x 11.4 cm) or the desired shape of your moist tile. Even with this loose technique, don't forget to calculate shrinkage. When cutting several textured tiles in this manner, alternate flat cuts with textured cuts in order not to waste any clay.

Right: Ellie Stein
Miriam and Her Tambourine. 1992
48" x 36" (121.9 x 91.4 cm)

Below: Beth Starbuck and Steven Goldner
Skybars & Trapezoids (detail). 1992
48" x 36" x 1" (121.9 x 91.4 x 2.5 cm)

After the tiles have been cut, try not to handle or bend them too much; they're usually still soft. Smooth off their rough top surfaces by running your finger along each one. If the clay is still too soft, wait awhile before doing this; you don't want the pressure from your finger to squish the tile.

Your tiles may look flat at this stage, but will they stay that way? Herein lies one of tile making's greatest challenges. In fact, the biggest problem most beginners have is getting their tiles to dry and fire flat. Though your tiles may never attain the flatness and perfection of commercial *dust-pressed* tiles, which are made by compressing dry clay particles with hydraulic machinery, that's not what handmade tiles are about. It's reasonable, however, to aim for a tile that isn't warped.

Drying the Tiles

Greenware, whether it is decorated with underglazes or not, must be dried before it can be fired. As you read this section, keep in mind that different decorative techniques for greenware are executed at different stages of dryness. Before you tackle these techniques, described in the next few chapters, you'll find it helpful to understand the tile-drying process.

When the clay is partly dry and as stiff as a thick piece of leather but contains some moisture and is still workable, it is called *leatherhard*. A leatherhard tile isn't flexible, but if you press your fingernail into its surface, the clay will retain an impression.

When the clay is *bone dry*, it will appear uniformly light in tone and will be dry to the touch. It will also be at room temperature and will rapidly absorb a drop of water placed on its surface. Bone-dry tiles are delicate and brittle, so handle them with care. And to avoid producing clay dust, don't scrape or sand them. Scraping and sanding are best executed on leatherhard tiles.

If tiles are left to dry rapidly on a wooden board, their upper, exposed surfaces usually dry faster (and shrink faster) than their bottom surfaces, and the tiles warp. Sculpted tiles' thinner edges may also dry at a different rate than their inner portions, causing warping as they do. Most shrinking and warping of tiles is a result of rapid moisture loss during the early drying stages; drying tiles slowly will help to prevent these problems.

One way to ensure slow drying at a controlled rate is to cover your tiles with a sheet of plastic for a day or so and then loosen the plastic so that air reaches the tiles slowly. While you're waiting for one project to dry and firm up, just tackle another. Or, if you're executing a decorative technique that is best completed on leatherhard tiles and you have a large batch of tiles to complete, you can keep them from becoming bone dry as you work on them one at a time. This will eliminate "down time" by allowing you to work on more than one project at a time.

The best method for producing really flat tiles, however, is to place rows of freshly cut tiles between layers of 1/2"-thick (1.3 cm) sheetrock or wallboard and then stack the boards in three or four layers (Photo 14). If you've cut your tile shapes from slabs placed on pieces of wallboard, all you'll need to do is stack these boards. The paper-covered plaster sheets absorb moisture evenly from both the tops and bottoms of the tiles, and the pressure created by the stacks helps to flatten the tiles. Avoid making the stacks too tall; the weight of too many tiles and boards may restrict shrinkage and cause undue stress. Of course, this method will only work for flat-surfaced tiles.

Don't cover these stacks with plastic unless you plan to be away for a few days and wish to prolong the drying process. When the tiles are in the latter stages of leatherhardness, they can be removed from the boards and set on a wooden shelf, another board, or any flat surface and left to continue drying in the open air, or they can be wrapped in plastic to maintain their leatherhard state. To help prevent warping, you may also stack the flat leatherhard tiles face to face, one tile upsidedown on top of another tile of the same shape.

You'll soon realize that success in working with clay is all in the timing. If you try to handle your tiles when they're still too soft, you will bend and squish and deform them. If you wait too long, the tiles may get too dry and brittle, and that certain technique that you wanted to try will no longer work.

CHAPTER FOUR

MAKING TILE MODELS
FOR OPEN-FACE PRESS MOLDS

Frank Giorgini
Floral. 1993
12" x 12" (30.5 x 30.5 cm)
Photograph by Bobby Hansson

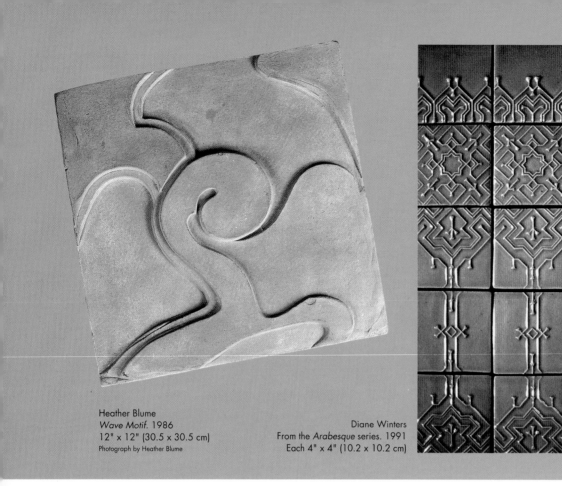

Heather Blume
Wave Motif. 1986
12" x 12" (30.5 x 30.5 cm)
Photograph by Heather Blume

Diane Winters
From the *Arabesque* series. 1991
Each 4" x 4" (10.2 x 10.2 cm)

Relief Tiles

Relief tiles, unlike the flat tiles described in chapter 3, are tiles with three-dimensional designs on their surfaces. Because designing and sculpting an original handmade relief tile takes a great deal of time and work, it makes sense to create an *open-face press mold* (a plaster mold of the original tile) with which you can press out multiple replicas of the tile.

Your single-tile design can be a complete composition in itself—one that is meant to stand alone—or can represent one unit or section of an overall graphic pattern that is formed when that unit is arranged with others exactly like it.

The original tile is a positive *model,* one that's used to make an open-face plaster mold and that is sometimes destroyed during the process. The mold will be a negative shell of the original positive tile model, and the tiles that are produced with the mold will be positive replicas of the original tile.

Tile models for the open-face press-mold process can be made in many ways; *layering* and *direct carving* are two.

The Layering Technique

The layering technique, one way to create a high-relief tile model for an open-face press mold, lends itself to hard-edged bold relief and graphic designs. Tiles made with this method usually look very sculptural and architectural.

First, you'll need to work out a design. Let's assume that you'd like to come up with a composition consisting of identical tile units that will be arranged next to one another. Following is a technique that may help you to visualize your overall design.

Draw a series of 2" x 2" (5.1 cm x 5.1 cm) squares on a piece of standard graph paper. Imagine that each of these squares is a single tile; you have as many chances to dream up a single-tile unit as you have squares on your page.

Next, draw a different design in each square. Remember that each square represents an entirely different design concept; you'll choose only one, which will then become the single-tile design upon which your composite design is eventually based. Keep the different designs simple and let one idea flow into another.

When you've filled the page, make ten to twelve photocopies of it. Then cut out each 2" (5.1 cm) square; you'll now have ten to twelve squares for each design that you created. In order to visualize your overall design, play with each set of identical squares, manipulating the individual squares to form a complete design. Take a look at Photo 15, in which you'll see a composite design in the lower left-hand corner; a single-tile unit is in my hand. You'll be surprised by how quickly patterns evolve with the various arrangements of these design units.

As you work with this technique, keep in mind that while your tiles don't have to be square, a square tile can be oriented in four different directions, a triangle in three, and a rectangle in only two. It's fun and informative to play with the tile cutouts this way.

Once you have selected a design, transfer it, enlarging it to its full size, onto another sheet of paper. It's easiest to do this on a photocopier, but it's also possible to do by hand. If your small tile cutout is 2" (5.1 cm)

Diane Winters
Geometric Rope. 1990
Each 3-3/4" x 3-3/4" (9.5 x 9.5 cm)

Decide how many layers your relief design will require; two or three levels are sufficient for most relief designs. You may find it helpful to color, shade, or otherwise mark each section of the finished pattern to designate that section's level. You'll notice that if two design areas of the same level are next to each other, they become a new shape—a combination of the two. You may therefore have to alter the designated levels so that each shape is defined by its vertical (relief) edges.

Next, roll out as many slabs of clay as there are layers in your design. For a three-layered design, roll two slabs that are each about 3/16" (.5 cm) thick and one slab about 3/8" (1.0 cm) thick. For a two-layered design, beginners might want to start with a 1/2"-thick (1.3 cm) bottom layer and 1/4"-thick (.6 cm) top layer. These slabs should be about 2" (5.1 cm) longer and 2" (5.1 cm) wider than the full size of the individual moist tile. If your tile design is 8-1/2" x 8-1/2" (21.6 cm x 21.6 cm), for example, each slab should be roughly 10-1/2" x 10-1/2" (26.7 cm x 26.7 cm).

To make a three-layered design, you'll stack the three slabs on top of one another and then carve away sections of each slab to create your relief design. Consider this fact before you decide whether to smooth off each slab's surface, leave the canvas texture on it, or roll another texture into it (see page 59). If the middle layer, for example, has a texture in it, once you've removed the uppermost layer, the texture will be visible.

After the slabs have set up for about thirty minutes and their surfaces are no longer sticky, layer them on top of each other, placing the thickest one on the bottom and setting the stack on a board that can be placed on a turntable.

square, for example, and you'd like your tile to be 8" (20.3 cm) square, draw a new square—one in which there are four graph units for every one unit in the old square—on a new sheet of graph paper. Then redraw the pattern into the new square by copying the contents of each small graph unit on the old sheet into each four-unit section on the new sheet. If you want your fired tile to be a specific size, don't forget to calculate and take into account the percentage of shrinkage.

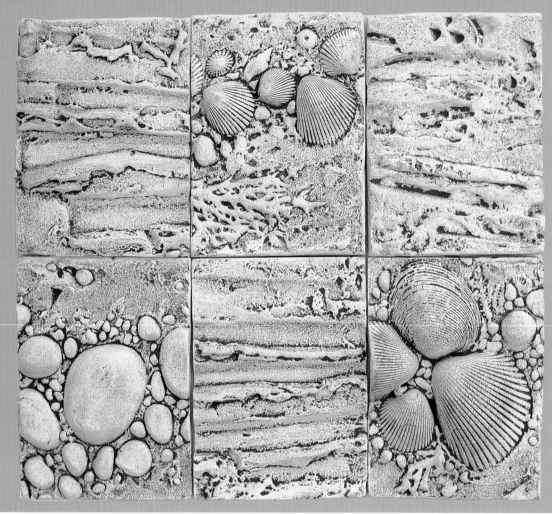

Hanna Lore Hombordy
Shells and Sand. 1991
14" x 16" (35.6 x 40.6 cm)
Photograph by Hanna Lore Hombordy

Next, center the sheet of graph paper with your full-sized tile design on the top of the layered pile, making sure that all four edges of each slab extend beyond the perimeter of the design. You wouldn't want to discover, after you'd trimmed the excess clay away, that your design stretched beyond the outer edge of one of the hidden slabs.

To transfer the design, use your pin tool to pierce through the graph paper along each design line (Photo 16). When a design line extends right to the edge of the tile's perimeter, visualize the line continuing beyond that perimeter and poke an additional hole into the slab out-side the perimeter. As you connect the inner dots by scribing over them, you may obliterate some; these outer dots will provide you with reference points if you do. Both the transferred design lines and reference-point dots are shown in Photo 17.

It's also possible to transfer your design by tracing over the paper pattern with a pencil; the pressure will leave a depression in the clay. This method, however, won't leave as clean an edge once you've cut along the line on the clay. A slight indentation may still be visible after you've sliced through the line's center. Now remove the graph paper, use a pin tool to connect the

Ellie Hudovernik
Sheep on Canopy Bed. 1993
6" x 6" (15.2 x 15.2 cm)
Photograph by Robert Hudovernik

Susan Beere
Egret's View. 1991
36" x 24" (91.4 x 61.0 cm)
Photograph by Hugh L. Wilkerson

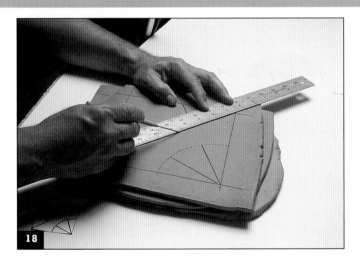

when the mold is poured and will make it impossible to release the clay model from the hard plaster mold. Thinking of your model as a series of pyramids may help. The edges of every level of the design should angle upward and inward. If you place a light directly

dots (Photo 18), and you're ready to cut. To make the cuts, use a knife with a fine blade. A No. 11 craft-knife blade will work well on all but the thickest tiles. For these, use any sharp, fine-bladed knife. As you cut the design into the tile model, the most important thing to remember is to avoid undercuts. The sides of each cut design section should be angled slightly outward—5° to 10° from perpendicular—so that each raised relief area is wider at its base than at its top surface. In Photo 19, note the angle at which I'm holding my knife. If the edges of the design's raised portions are angled incorrectly (inward), the undercut areas will fill with plaster

Opposite page, left:
Reneé Habert and Jim Stonebraker
Rabbit/Dog. 1993
9" x 9" (22.9 x 22.9 cm)
Photograph by Bobby Hansson

Opposite page, right: Arnon Zadok
City Tile. 1987
4" x 4" (10.2 x 10.2 cm)
Photograph by Bobby Hansson

Left: Beth Starbuck and Steven Goldner
Pinwheel Pentagons (detail). 1986
50" x 36" (127.0 x 91.4 cm)

Below: Frank Giorgini
Dark Dawn. 1985
Mounted mural: 28" x 42"
(71.1 x 106.7 cm)
Photograph by John Lawrence

over the model, no shadow should appear on any edge of the design.

Hold the knife just as you would hold a pen. Rather than shifting your hand to make cuts on different portions of the tile, just spin the turntable so that—for right-handed people—the design area is always on your right. Grip the knife rigidly, keeping it at the proper 5° to 10° angle, and draw it towards you as you cut. Locking your hand, wrist, and arm into a rigid position and moving your whole body backwards will help you to control the knife; it's surprisingly easy to cut a straight line at a constant angle when you use this method. Practice helps, of course!

Cut the perimeter of the tile first and then the inscribed lines of the interior design. Keep checking the angle of your knife so as not to undercut. If you're right-handed and are cutting lines on the left side of the stacked slabs, the top of the knife blade should be angled slightly toward the right. In more complicated designs, the directions of the angles can get tricky, but once you understand the principle of layering, you'll have no trouble figuring them out. To facilitate cutting curved lines, keep your knife stationary and rotate the turntable instead.

Don't worry about accidentally cutting too deeply into the lower layer while you slice through the one above it. Unless you slice all the way through the lower layer, these accidental cuts are not a problem. They'll leave thin fins of plaster on your mold, but these fins are easy to remove. The real problem comes from not cutting deeply enough, which will create a ragged, torn edge when you remove the layers.

Now comes the exciting part. Starting with the top layer, poke into the exposed edge of a design section that needs to be removed and then carefully peel it away. Once you've removed the unwanted sections from the top layer, use the same cutting-and-peeling

20

method to remove the unwanted sections from the middle layer (Photo 20), working down toward the base layer, which should remain uncut unless you plan to create a hole in your tile. Remember, each edge of each section that remains should angle downward and outward from its own top surface.

Though the layering technique just described lends itself to hard-edged geometric designs, it can also serve as a basic starting point for any type of relief design. If you'd like to create a realistic animal figure, for instance, begin with three stacked slabs and then carve and round them off. This method will help you to get a feel for carving in relief. (The *Rabbit/Dog* tile shown above was made in this manner.)

Your clay model is now ready to cast into a plaster mold. Because you haven't wet, scored, and adhered the layers of this model together as you would have if you were direct carving a single tile for firing, the layers would separate if they were dried and fired. The model that you've just made, however, won't be dried or fired. Instead, it will be discarded after you've made a mold with it. See the next chapter for mold-making instructions.

Frank Giorgini
Vine with Parrot. 1993
12" x 12"
(30.5 x 30.5 cm)
Photograph by Bobby Hansson

Heather Blume
Frog Tile. 1992
4" x 3" (10.2 x 7.6 cm)
Photograph by Heather Blume

The Direct Carving Technique

In direct carving, the moist clay model is actually sculpted. Similar models can be made with wax or oil-based clay, neither of which will shrink as you work with them. If you enjoy working with moist earthen clay and are accustomed to it, however, you might prefer to stick with it. Do remember not to mix oil-based clay and water-based clay; the results would be disastrous.

Once you've selected a design, transfer it onto a rolled-out slab of clay. The slab should be wider and longer than your design, because you'll be whittling away at it. In fact, you will need to add even more clay to the amount that is necessary after shrinkage has been taken into account. If your finished tile will be 4" x 4" (10.2 cm x 10.2 cm), for example, and shrinkage calls for a 4-1/2" x 4-1/2" (11.4 cm x 11.4 cm) moist tile, roll out a 5-1/2" x 5-1/2" (14.0 cm x 14.0 cm) slab.

Because you'll be adding clay to this tile, as well as removing it, roll your slab to about three-quarters the thickness of your finished tile; the cut slab should be about as thick as the middle ground of your design.

Now scrape clay away from the background areas and build up the elevated areas by adding more moist clay. Mastering the layering technique described in the previous section will help you to visualize the transformation of a two-dimensional paper design into a three-dimensional bas-relief tile. A tile at three stages of direct carving is shown in Photo 21.

For scraping, pushing, and shaping the clay into the desired shapes and contours, use various bamboo or wooden *sculpting tools*, *scraping tools* such as mat-knife blades and sections of hacksaw blades, and *looped trimming tools*. (In chapter 14, you'll find directions for making some of these tools yourself.) Dental tools are useful for creating fine details; ask your dentist if he or she has any available.

When you're building up areas of the tile, always score the slab's surface with a pin tool, add a little water or clay slip (which acts as a glue) to the scored

21

surface, and then press the additional moist clay on top. (See page 62 for a description of clay slip.) Be sure to press the added clay down well; you don't want to trap any air between the upper and lower pieces. You can make a slip that shrinks at the same rate as your tile model by collecting the little scraps that you trim off tiles made with the same clay. Let these scraps dry to bone dry, put them in a plastic bucket, and mix them with some water. The result will be a slip of the same composition as your clay body.

When the clay is too soft, only rough shaping (the first stage of sculpting) is possible. To make the clay more workable, cover the model with plastic and let it set up overnight. As it loses moisture and approaches leatherhard, refining its surface design will be easier.

After you've completed your tile model, keep it under plastic until you are ready to mold it. To keep it in its leatherhard state, just spritz it intermittently with water. If you let the clay get bone dry, you'll find it difficult to return it to its leatherhard state, so keep an eye on it. As long as beads of moisture are forming under the plastic, the tile is sufficiently moist.

The next step is to make an open-face press mold from your layered or carved model.

CHAPTER FIVE

MAKING AND USING
OPEN-FACE PRESS MOLDS

George Mason
Variation. 1991
34" x 34" (86.4 x 86.4 cm)
Photograph by Dennis Griggs

George Johnson
Table and Bench. 1993
Table: 72" x 36"
(182.9 x 91.4 cm)
Bench: 36" x 36"
(91.4 x 91.4 cm)
Photograph by Bobby Hansson

Preparing the Model and Form

Now that you've created a tile model, the next step in the open-face press-mold process is to make a plaster mold. You'll do this by assembling a form around your model, mixing plaster, and pouring it into the form.

First, transfer your leatherhard model from the surface where it was shaped to a smooth, nonporous surface. Place the edge of a wooden ruler on one side of the tile and gently push the tile off onto a thick piece of glass or Formica. Secure the model by gently pressing it in place. If the model is too dry and seems to slide on the smooth surface, just dampen its back a little with a sponge and then press it down again. If the model doesn't adhere properly to the surface, the force of pouring the plaster over it may cause it to shift its position.

In order to contain the liquid plaster mixture that you'll pour over your model, you'll need to build a *plaster mold form* to place around it (Photo 22). These forms are referred to as *cottles* (or walls) and are made from wood or plastic. They are held together with C-clamps, straps, or threaded rods. (For instructions on how to make a plaster mold form, see chapter 14.) The cottles must be high enough and sturdy enough to contain the plaster, and you must be able to adjust them to fit the tile. To calculate the height of the form, add 1-1/2" to 2" (3.8 cm to 5.1 cm) to the depth of the highest surface of the clay model. Pieces of standard 2 x 4 are often suitable; their 3-1/2" (8.9 cm) width provides a convenient form height.

Adjust your mold form to leave about 1-1/2" to 2" (3.8 cm to 5.1 cm) between each side of the tile model and the inside surfaces of the form. Secure the form and seal all its corners by pressing a thin coil of clay along its inside bottom edges and into its inside corners (Photo 23). If you're using deep-walled cottles, make a reference mark in the soft clay in one corner, about 1" (2.5 cm) above the highest part of your model. This mark

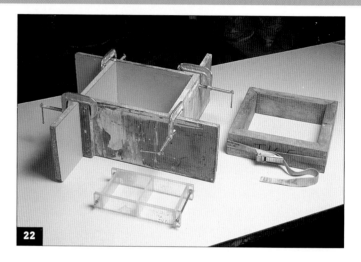

22

23

will tell you how much more plaster to add once the model itself has been submerged.

Next, you may need to coat the working surface and the inside surfaces of the form with a *release* (a substance that will prevent the plaster from sticking). Mold

Cynthia Lyons
Trout Tile. 1993
6" x 6" (15.2 x 15.2 cm)
Photograph by Cynthia Lyons

Dale Wiley
Mola. 1988
6-5/8" x 6-5/8" (16.8 x 16.8 cm)
Photograph by Peter von Wilken Zook

soap, petroleum jelly, vegetable oils, and spray lubricants will all work. Plaster won't stick to clay, so you won't have to apply release to the model itself. Clean glass, Formica, and varnished wood release very well with a minimum of lubricant, but a surface like unfinished wood requires a generous coating of release.

After you've secured your tile model on the glass, adjusted your form around it, and sealed and coated the inside of the form with a release, you'll be ready to create a negative mold of your work by mixing and pouring plaster into the form.

Mixing and Pouring the Plaster

Plaster (a powdered, semi-hydrated form of gypsum which, when mixed with water, recrystallizes to a hardened state) is the preferred material for mold making. Interestingly, the term *Plaster of Paris* is derived from the first recorded use of plaster by potters, in early eighteenth-century France.

Contemporary tile makers often use industrial-quality *potter's No. 1 plaster*. This material can be obtained from your clay supply distributor; it comes in 50-pound (22.7 kg) and 100-pound (45.4 kg) bags. Be sure to store plaster in a dry place; its shelf life is limited by its tendency to absorb moisture.

Hydracal is another, stronger molding material, one often used by advanced tile makers. This substance can be used alone or mixed with plaster in a one-to-one ratio. A mold made with Hydracal will be stronger than one made with plaster but will also be less absorbent, so your tile will not release from the mold as quickly.

To calculate the necessary amount of plaster, first refer to Chart I, which provides rough sizes for mold forms and the necessary amounts of water and plaster to mix for each form. Use the water weights as your reference. The plaster weights are accurate, and it's a good idea to have at least as much dry plaster on hand

as the chart indicates is necessary, but the plaster-mixing method that you are about to learn doesn't require you to premeasure the plaster that you use. You'll be gauging the amount of plaster by eye, instead, in a technique known as the *"island" method*.

Note in this chart that the amounts of plaster and water are based on the amount of mixed plaster required to fill an empty mold form. Your tile model will displace some of the mixed plaster, so you'll have some plaster left over.

Chart I

Plaster Mixing

Size of Mold-Form Interior	Pounds (Kg) of Water	Pounds (Kg) of Plaster
8" x 8" x 3" (20.3 cm x 20.3 cm x 7.6 cm)	4.5 (2.0 kg)	7 (3.2 kg)
9" x 9" x 3" (22.9 cm x 22.9 cm x 7.6 cm)	6 (2.7 kg)	9 (4.1 kg)
10" x 10" x 3" (25.4 cm x 25.4 cm x 7.6 cm)	7 (3.2 kg)	11 (5.0 kg)
11" x 11" x 3" (27.9 cm x 27.9 cm x 7.6 cm)	9 (4.1 kg)	13.5 (6.1 kg)
12" x 12" x 3" (30.5 cm x 30.5 cm x 7.6 cm)	10.5 (4.8 kg)	16 (7.3 kg)
13" x 13" x 3" (33.0 cm x 33.0 cm x 7.6 cm)	13 (5.9 kg)	19.5 (8.6 kg)
14" x 14" x 3" (35.6 cm x 35.6 cm x 7.6 cm)	14 (6.4 kg)	21 (9.5 kg)
15" x 15" x 3" (38.1 cm x 38.1 cm x 7.6 cm)	17 (7.7 kg)	26 (11.8 kg)
16" x 16" x 3" (40.6 cm x 40.6 cm x 7.6 cm)	20 (9.1 kg)	30 (13.6 kg)

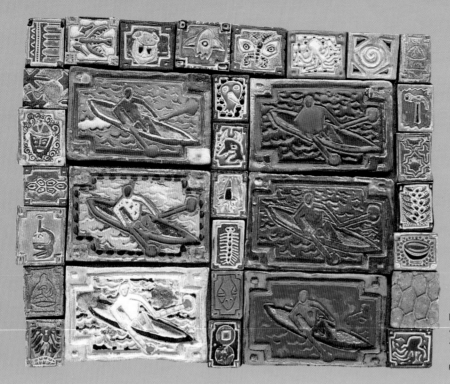

The ratio of plaster to water determines the strength and absorbency of your finished mold. A standard mixture is about 100 parts water to 140 parts plaster. Specific technical formulas and charts are available for mixing plaster, but for our purposes, the age-old island method will work just fine. Here's how to use it.

Place the required amount of cold tap water in a clean plastic bucket. The bucket should not only be large enough to hold the required amount of water and plaster, but should also leave you ample space for stirring and mixing the two together. Adding plaster to the water will increase the volume of the bucket's contents by about 50%. If the bucket is filled to 6" (15.2 cm) with water, for example, adding the plaster will raise the level of the contents to about 9" (22.9 cm).

Before you begin to mix in the plaster, you should have on hand a water-tight receptacle or another prepared form; you'll need to pour any leftover plaster into one of these containers so that it doesn't harden in the bucket. You should also mix up a 1/2-cup (118.4 ml) test batch (see the mixing instructions that follow). Wait to see how this small batch of plaster sets up; if it never gets hard, throw your dry plaster away and begin again with a fresh bag. Plaster can become stale if it lies around the studio for a long time.

You'll only have about one to four minutes pouring time, depending upon the condition of your plaster mixture, so be sure to prepare your model and mold forms before you begin. While wearing a dust mask and rubber gloves, sprinkle the plaster steadily across the entire surface of the water in the bucket, allowing the plaster to sink as you do. If the plaster has lumps in it, sift it through a 20-mesh screen as you pour it in.

Continue to add plaster until islands of plaster begin to form above the water's surface. Stop sprinkling until the islands are absorbed and then add a little

more. Wait again for the islands to be absorbed and add more. These waiting periods are called *slaking*; tap the bucket during slaking in order to make any air bubbles rise to the surface. At first, the islands will sink into the water very quickly. As you continue, however, they'll take longer and longer to be absorbed. Stop adding plaster as soon as the islands sit for ten to fifteen seconds before they're absorbed.

Then mix the solution carefully, using your fingers to squeeze out any lumps. To avoid creating air bubbles, keep your gloved hands submerged. Continue blending until the mixture is the consistency of light cream. You'll have a minute or so to complete the mixing; don't panic, but do work at a steady pace. As soon as the plaster turns from a light cream consistency to a heavy cream consistency, it's time to pour it.

Pour the plaster into the mold form slowly and steadily, aiming for the area between the tile model and form and letting the plaster flow slowly over the model (Photo 24). Fill the form to the desired thickness, about 1" to 1-1/2" (2.5 cm to 3.8 cm) above the model's upper-

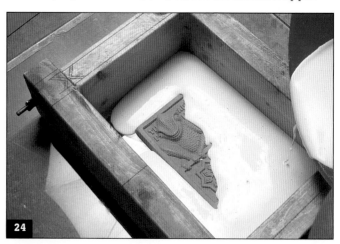

24

most surface. Jiggling the table gently will help the plaster to settle into the model's nooks and crannies and will also release any trapped air bubbles. Pour the excess plaster into the extra form or waterproof container.

Don't worry if the plaster that you've mixed is a little thin. Your mold will just take a little longer than usual to dry. Plaster that's too thick is more problematic; it will begin to harden before you get a chance to pour it and will flow out in gobs as you do. Plaster this thick won't pick up fine details from your tile model.

Cleaning Up and Finishing the Mold

Wipe the excess plaster on the sides of the bucket down toward the bottom. Immediately add about a cup (236.8 ml) of water and rinse the inside of the bucket by swishing its contents around. Then pour the contents into the waterproof container, where they'll settle to a semihard state and can be disposed of along with solid waste. (Pouring the rinse down the sink would clog the drain.) Now sponge and rinse your mixing bucket thoroughly. If you wait to clean it, any remaining plaster will harden, and the bucket will be very difficult to clean.

You'll notice that plaster gives off heat as it hardens; this is a result of the recrystallization process. After it has reached its highest temperature and has hardened (in thirty to forty-five minutes), remove the mold forms and then scrape and clean them.

Slide the hardened plaster mold off the glass surface and flip it over so that the bottom of your clay tile model is visible. Gently peel out the soft clay (Photo 25), using a wooden tool, if necessary, to lift the edge of the model from the mold. Be careful not to nick the inside of the mold. You'll probably have to discard the clay model, but you'll now have an exact, negative plaster replica of your tile. By filling its negative space with moist clay, you can make literally hundreds of replicas of your original tile.

To dry the mold, first place a couple of sticks—uniform in size—on a drying shelf or board. Then place the mold on the sticks, with its negative (hollowed) side facing down. The mold may take a week to dry sufficiently. To accelerate the drying process, place the mold in a warm dry place or in front of a fan.

When the mold is completely dry, round off all its outside corners with a rasp; rounded edges are less likely to chip. They also look neater and make people think that you know what you're doing. Make sure that the back of the mold is smooth and flat.

On the mold's inside surfaces, you may notice thin fins of plaster sticking up out of your design. These are

created when plaster flows into deep cuts left in the clay by your knife. Just break the fins off with your fingers. Use a wooden tool for any other trimming, but don't rush to do too much. It's better to press out your first tile replica and then determine if other adjustments to the mold really need to be made.

Making Clay Plugs for the Open-Face Press Mold

The next step is to press moist clay into the negative mold and pop out a positive replica of your original tile model. Start by dusting out the dry plaster mold with a clean, soft brush. Place it face up on a smooth, 3/4"-thick (1.9 cm) bed of unwrinkled newspapers or flat cardboard; folded ridges in the newspaper or cardboard bed may cause the mold to crack when you pound on it.

Then make a *plug* (or slab) of soft clay that is a little thicker than the deepest part of your mold and just large enough to fit into the opening in it. Just use the slab-cutting and rolling method described in chapter 3.

If you plan to make many plugs of the same size, you may want to use a *slab cutter* to cut them (Photo 26).

thick slabs from a newly opened bag of clay, making it unnecessary to roll out clay slabs with a rolling pin or slab roller, a process that often takes longer than it does to press the tile itself.

To use the slab cutter, begin by slamming four sides of a sealed bag of moist clay down onto your work table until the top end of the clay block is roughly the size of the desired plug. Then place the bag on end and carefully peel back the plastic. Position the slab cutter face down on the clay and draw the taut wire towards you by pulling it along the protruding metal or wooden edges. The wire will slice off a clay slab of uniform thickness. Remove the slab and place it on a piece of canvas. Repeat this process until the entire block has been sliced into plugs.

Next, using a pin tool and a template that is just the size of the opening in the mold, cut each plug to shape. Then wedge up the trimmings and cut a few more plugs from them. Stack the plugs, placing pieces of canvas between the layers. Cover the stack with plastic so that the tiles are kept moist until you're ready to use them. By first forming clay plugs in the correct sizes and thicknesses, you can press out tiles faster and more efficiently.

Pressing the Plugs into the Mold

Place a plug in the mold (Photo 27) and tap it down gently with the palm of your hand, working from the cen-

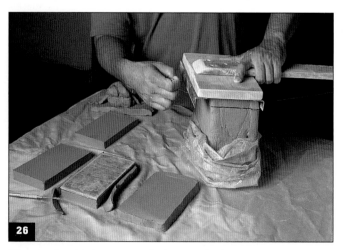

This tool, which can easily be made from scrap materials (see chapter 14 for instructions), will cut your preparation time in half when you're cutting multiple slabs of identical thicknesses. It operates by cutting uniformly

ter to the corners and making sure that the plug fills the mold's edges and corners. Then place a piece of cut canvas over the clay and pound the clay down by striking the canvas with a rubber mallet (Photo 28). Again, try to make sure that you're forcing the clay into the edges and corners. (Use clean canvas if you can. If your canvas has dry clay residue on it, mist the surface with water to keep the dust from rising as you pound with the mallet.)

along the mold's top surface (Photo 30). This will remove the excess clay fairly close to the mold's back surface. To smooth off the surface even more, take a rigid, straight

Next, place a small block of wood on top of the canvas and really wallop it down with the mallet (Photo 29). Move it to another area above the mold opening and hit it again. Repeat this process until the entire area has been pounded into the mold. Be careful not to hit your fingers.

After you've packed the clay into the mold, fold up the squashed-out clay edges. Stretch your cut-off wire taut between your hands and draw it back toward you,

Nawal and Karim Motawi
Old English Rabbit. 1993
6" x 6" (15.2 x 15.2 cm)
Photograph by Nawal Motawi

Frank Giorgini
Rhino. 1993
6" x 6" (15.2 x 15.2 cm)
Photograph by Bobby Hansson

stick and scrape it across the surface of the tile (Photo 31). Work from the middle of the tile toward the edges, or you'll distort the clay by pulling it away from the edges of the mold opening. When the stick passes smoothly across the entire surface, the back of your tile is flat.

Now is the time to incise or stamp your name or logo into the back of the tile. Then place a smooth block of plaster (the back of another mold or a couple of pieces of wallboard will do) over the top of the mold and set it aside to dry. The weight of the plaster block on top and the plaster surrounding the clay will help the tile to dry and shrink evenly. (For instructions on how to make plaster blocks, see chapter 14.)

Depending on the condition of the mold and on the complexity of your design, the tile should be ready for removal between fifteen minutes and an hour later. Simple, open, shallow designs will release more quickly than complex, deep ones. Check the mold periodically. When the clay's edges start to separate from the mold, your tile can be released. In most cases, the tile shouldn't be allowed to dry completely in the mold because it will shrink and crack around the mold's solid, raised sections.

To remove the tile, place two narrow strips of wood or corner molding, approximately 1/4" (.6 cm) thick, on

the edges of the mold, making sure that the strips don't cover the clay tile. Then place a sturdy board (face down) on the wooden strips, flip the whole assembly over, and tap the top of the mold.

The tile may slip right out (Photo 32), but it's more likely that you'll have to exert a little force to help it along. Tap the mold's edges, above the wood strips, with a rubber mallet. Don't hit the middle of the mold or you might crack it. If this doesn't release the tile, try lifting one edge of the board up about 2" (5.1 cm) and slamming it down onto a sturdy table. This procedure could raise some dust, so keep all your tools and equipment clean.

Keep peeking into the space between the board and the mold to see whether the tile has fallen out of the mold on all sides. Once it has, remove the mold and the sticks and press the tile gently down to make sure that it's lying flat. Tapping the board down on the table will also settle the tile down flat. You now have an exact replica of your original tile model.

Next, transfer the tile to a piece of wallboard to dry. Push it onto the board by gently pressing against a length of wood placed against the side of the tile. The tile can be left to dry at this point. If it warps, refer to pages 34 and 54 for techniques that will help you to avoid this problem in the future.

CHAPTER SIX

CARVED PLASTER BLOCKS, TILE PRESSES, AND EXTRUDERS

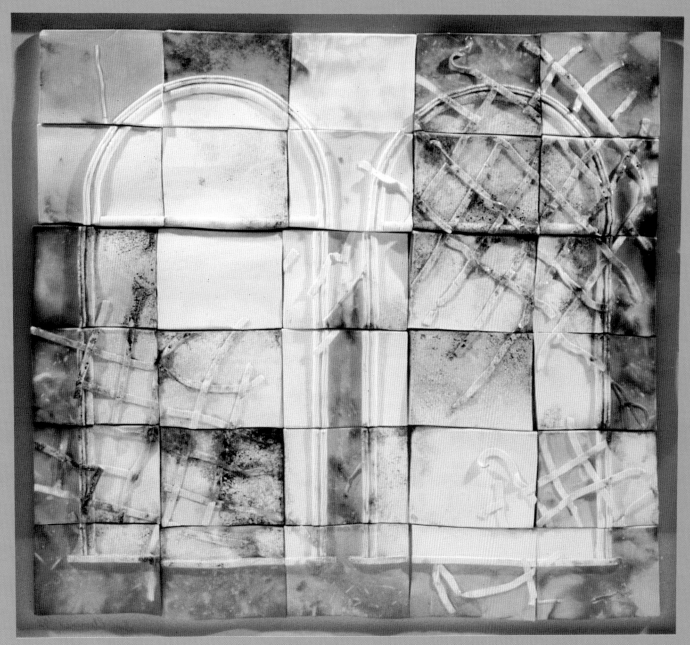

Carol Susan Clemens
Two Day. 1992
17" x 22" (43.2 x 55.9 cm)

Making a Carved Plaster Block

This method of pressing out a tile differs from that described in the previous chapter in that the negative design is sculpted directly into a plaster block; no tile model is necessary (Photo 33). In addition, tiles made with the carved-block technique, unlike those made with an open-face press mold, do not need to dry and shrink before they're released from the block. For these two reasons, the carved-block method is considerably faster, especially if you use a tile press instead of pressing the tiles by hand.

Note also that a carved block is as long and as wide as the actual tile that you press with it. Unlike the flat border area of an open-face press mold, which serves only as a restraint, the flat area of a carved plaster block is an active part of your tile design; the flat background of your tile will be pressed by it. The raised relief sections of your finished tile will be shaped by the block's carved sections.

First, you'll need to make a block of hardened plaster, about 1-1/2" (3.8 cm) thick and shaped to the desired size of your tile before (not after) shrinkage. For instruc-

tions on how to make several of these blocks at one time, see chapter 14.

Tools for scraping and gouging, such as those used in linoleum-block cutting and engraving, are useful, as are looped trimming tools, a pin tool, and a knife.

There are several ways to transfer your design to the surface of the plaster block. The method that you choose will depend in part on whether your design is symmetrical or asymmetrical. If the design is symmetrical, just draw or trace it directly onto the block. An asymmetrical design—one that incorporates letters or numbers, for example—will have to be transferred in reverse as a mirror image of the original design. One way to do this is to first use a soft pencil to draw the design on paper. Then flip the paper over, place it face down over the block, and rub over the back of the paper to transfer the graphite pencil markings to the surface of the white block.

A similar transferring technique is shown in Photos 34, 35, and 36. First, copy the design to the correct size on a commercial photocopy machine. Place the copy on the block with its printed side

Opposite page:
Diane Winters
Iris and *Dianthus.*
1992
Each 4" x 4"
(10.2 x 10.2 cm)

Right: Lloyd Reiss
Reflection. 1993
5-1/2" x 5-1/2"
and 6" x 6"
(14.0 x 14.0 cm
and 15.2 x 15.2 cm)
Photograph by Bobby Hansson

35

36

Next, carve the design. Remember that the areas you carve away will appear as raised sections on the surface of your pressed tile. If you find this concept visually confusing, check your progress as you carve by periodically pressing a wad of soft clay into the surface of the plaster block (Photo 37). In general, carve down a maximum of about half the thickness of the background tile base. If you're carving relatively deeply, keep the

37

grooves wide enough to allow the clay to be pressed all the way down into them.

It's possible to make a similar press block from bisqued clay instead of from plaster by incising or impressing a low-relief design into a leatherhard tile and then bisque firing it. This bisqued tile can be used to press soft clay tiles; their designs will be mirror images of the original tile design. The photos at the top of this page show the results of this technique. Plaster-block molds are stronger than these pressing tiles, and the clay will release more easily from them, but if you want to avoid working with plaster and have limited production in mind, using a pressing tile can be an adequate alternative.

facing down. Then dab the back of the copy with a ball of cotton that has been wetted with nail-polish remover. (Use nonacetone removers only; they're much less hazardous to your health.) The copy-machine ink will transfer right onto the block. Unfortunately, this method doesn't work as well on leatherhard clay as it does on plaster.

Opposite page: Diane Winters
Untitled. 1990
Each 5" x 5" (12.7 x 12.7 cm)

Left: Diana and Tom Watson
Design by Sussman Prejza
*Leo Palace Resort:
Daro Road Sign.* 1993
36" x 312" (91.4 x 792.5 cm)
Photograph by Bielenberg

Pressing Tiles by Hand

There are two ways to use your carved plaster block to create the relief surface on your tile: pressing by hand and mallet and pressing with a tile press, a tool that is described in the next section.

To press your tiles by hand, first place the carved block face up on a cushioning bed of newspapers. Then cut a slab of clay that's the same length and width as the block; you can trace around the block itself. The thickness of the slab should be slightly greater than the thickness of your finished tile, including its relief portions. For a very shallow relief—1/8" (.3 cm), for example—the slab shouldn't be much thicker than the finished tile. For a 3/8"-deep (1.0 cm) carved design, the slab might 1/2" (1.3 cm) thick. If you find that your slab is too thin, just roll out one that's a little thicker.

Next, place the slab over the block and position a piece of canvas on top of the slab. Then, on top of the canvas, place a wooden board that's about the same width and length as the plaster block. If the board is too large, you'll have a difficult time keeping it level as you pound it. If your carved block is exceptionally large, perhaps 18" (45.7 cm) or longer, use a small wooden block first, moving it around the surface as you pound, but finish up with a large block.

Tap the wooden block down with a mallet so that the resulting tile is of uniform thickness. When the tile is the desired thickness, trim away the excess clay by running your pin around the block's perimeter. Then carefully peel the tile from the block, trying not to bend it as you do. You should have an exact positive impression of your carved design (Photo 38).

38

Place your pressed tiles on a board or piece of wallboard, cover them with plastic, and let them dry for a day or so. To complete the drying, gradually pull back the plastic, letting more and more air get to the tiles. (Drying boxes can be purchased, but it's easier to build a wooden frame and surround it with plastic instead.)

A variation on the carved-block technique is shown in Photo 39. The plaster blocks on the left-hand side of this photo were actually cast right from the surface of a relief pattern. Like a carved block, a mold cast in this manner is the same width and length as the moist clay tile that is pressed with it. In the example shown, a plastic replica of an architectural molding was cut to about 6" (15.2 cm) in length. Cottles were set up flush with the edges of the plastic model, the mold was sealed with moist clay from the outside (not the inside), and the plaster was mixed

and poured as explained in chapter 5. Tile designs sculpted from moist clay can also be cast in this manner, and the molds that result also work well in a tile press.

Both the carved-block technique and the variation just described are most appropriate for smaller tiles—approximately 20 square inches (129.0 sq. cm) or less—the relief designs of which are low. For deeper, larger tiles and those with raised borders around the edges of their designs (see Photo 32 on page 50), make an open-face mold instead. If you attempted to create a tile border by using a carved block, you would have to carve a negative depression along the rim of your plaster block. Then, when you tried to use the block to press moist clay, the clay would tend to ooze out around the edges of the block; there would be no restraining border of plaster to force the clay back into the carved design

areas. For this reason, the open-face mold technique is better suited for tiles with borders.

Using a Tile Press

Combining the carved-block technique with the use of a hand-operated *tile press* provides a very quick and efficient method of producing detailed relief tiles. Studio tile presses are available commercially—there are even hydraulic studio models—but the hand-operated tile press shown in Photo 40 is one that I designed and built

Fired Earth Tiles
Fossil: Aquamarine. On-going
Each 4-5/16" x 4-5/16" x 3/8"
(11.0 x 11.0 x .9 cm)

myself. Instructions for making one just like it can be found in chapter 14. The simple lever-and-vertical-plunger design allows the user to apply an incremental amount of pressure to the block—evenly, quickly, and efficiently. The press can be also be used with open-face press molds, but the tile size should be limited to 20 square inches (129.0 sq. cm) or less.

To use the tile press, place a board on the base of the press and cover it with a piece of canvas. Place the slab of clay on the canvas and the carved block (face down) on the clay. On top of the block, position a layer of cardboard to serve as a cushion. Be sure to center the block and clay under the plunger. Then pull down once on the tile-press plunger, pressing the block down into the clay until the tile is the desired thickness. Turn the board and everything on it around 180° and pull the plunger down again. Doing this will help to compensate for the inevitable variations in pressure.

When you're making multiple tiles with the tile press, establishing a rhythm to your movements can speed up the process considerably. Pull the board out from under the plunger, remove the cardboard, and use your pin tool to trim the excess clay from the perimeter of the block. Pick up the block and peel the pressed tile off it. Then set the block aside and place the tile on a board, pressing the tile down gently to make sure that it's flat. Bend the tile as little as possible during this process. Return to the press and start again. The quick process of pressing, trimming, and releasing each tile from the block will enable you to really crank out the tiles.

At a certain point, the carved block will begin to get moist, and peeling the tiles from it will begin to be more difficult. When this happens, dry the block in front of a fan and take a break, or use another block while you let the damp one dry for fifteen or twenty minutes. Letting your clay slabs dry out for a few minutes before pressing the carved block into them will also help to keep the clay from sticking. Don't let them get too stiff, or pressing will be too difficult.

When the pressed tiles are leatherhard, trim their rough edges with a trimming tool. Then, using a damp sponge, stroke outward to smooth away any scrape marks.

Extruders

An *extruder* (Photo 41) is a tool that squeezes moist clay through a die in order to produce a relief design.

The tool includes a lever-and-plunger mechanism, a *barrel* (or chamber) into which the moist clay is placed, and interchangeable dies, each with a specific pattern cut through it. Dies for basic studio-model extruders are cut into plywood, plastic, or metal.

41

To operate the extruder, follow the manufacturer's directions. The basic process is simple. Fill the barrel with clay, select and attach a die to the bottom of the barrel, place the plunger and lever on top of the tool, and pull down on the lever. The pressure in the barrel forces moist clay through the shaped opening in the die. The linear form that is extruded can be cut at spaced intervals to yield individual tiles.

This tool is especially useful for making moldings, *bullnose edges* (to wrap around outside corners), inside corners, and flat tiles with a linear-relief surface design. With the right die in place, the extruder can even produce hollow shapes such as tubes or pipes. *Quarry tiles,* the floor tiles often seen in business environments, are usually produced by large hydraulic extruders in the tile industry. The upper surfaces of these tiles are flat and their bottom surfaces are ribbed; the ribbing helps the tiles to dry flat and to adhere better once they're installed.

CHAPTER SEVEN

SURFACE DECORATION ON UNFIRED TILES

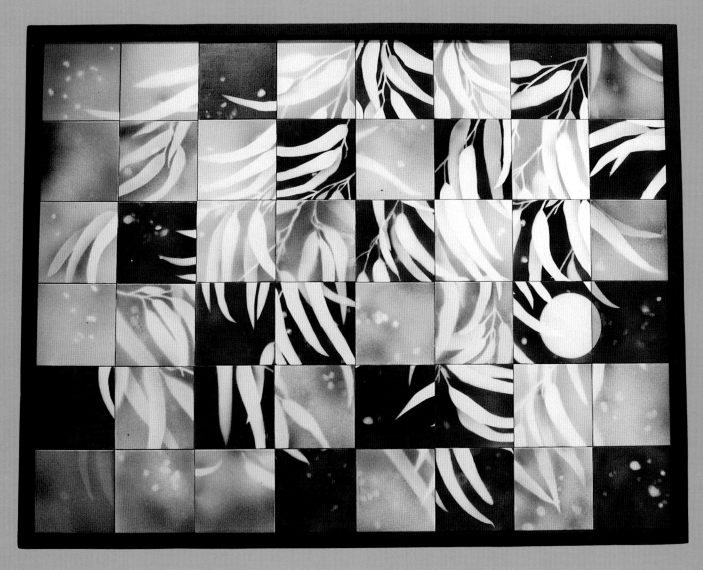

Hanna Lore Hombordy
Evening Breezes. 1991
26" x 35" (66.0 x 88.9 cm)
Photograph by Hanna Lore Hombordy

Linda R. Ellett
Geometric Pattern (detail). 1989
Each 5" x 5" (12.7 x 12.7 cm)
Photograph by Linda R. Ellett

Linda R. Ellett
Geometric Pattern (detail). 1989
Each 5" x 5" (12.7 x 12.7 cm)
Photograph by Linda R. Ellett

Stages of Tile Dryness

In this chapter, you'll find information on decorative techniques that are performed before your flat or relief tiles are bisque fired. Some of these methods work best on clay in its moist state, others on clay at the leatherhard stage, and still others on bone-dry clay. Appendix B on page 137 offers some guidelines as to when each of these techniques should be executed.

Transferring the Design

There are a number of ways to transfer your design to an unfired tile, some of which have already been discussed. One method is to use a pencil to draw the design right onto the leatherhard or bone-dry tile. Pencil lines on greenware will usually burn off in the firing. If the tile is still a little soft and has not yet reached the advanced leatherhard or bone-dry stage, however, your pencil point will probably leave an indentation in the tile's surface. This may, or may not, be desirable.

Special *underglaze pencils* that won't burn off, as well as pastel *underglaze crayons* (usually for use on bisque ware), are available. The crayons are actually underglazes in a nonliquid form; they may be used on greenware, on top of a painted underglaze, or on unglazed bisque.

You can also use tracing paper to trace the design onto a tile in its leatherhard stage. Place the paper (face up) on the tile and trace over it with a dull pointed tool; a pin tool or blunt pencil will work. The tool will impress a line into the soft clay or, as is shown in Photo 42, into a coat of underglaze that has already been applied to the tile.

A fourth method for transferring designs involves piercing holes in the design lines on your paper in order to leave dots in the leatherhard clay. One disadvantage to this technique is that it will leave visible dots in the clay surface.

42

Yet another method—a traditional one known as *pouncing*—involves making pin pricks along the design lines on a piece of paper. After the pierced paper has been positioned on the tile, a small cloth bag filled with finely ground charcoal is "pounced" over the pierced holes. The design lines are thus transferred in the form of dots of charcoal dust. In spite of its messiness, this technique is reliable.

Impressing

One of the wonderful properties of clay is its malleability; when it's moist, any object that is pressed into it will leave an impression. At different stages of stiffening, from soft and moist to leatherhard, the tile will exhibit different levels of impression sharpness. Impressing is an effective method of adding interesting three dimensionality to your tile's surface.

Many objects make good impressions: letters and numbers from old type sets, children's plastic alphabet sets, carved wooden or plaster shapes, and rubber stamps. (Logos can be made into stamps relatively inexpensively.) Natural objects—leaves, shells, seeds,

Jane W. Larson
Energy and Life (detail of
Chlorophyll panel). 1992
36" x 360" x 2"
(91.4 x 914.4 x 5.1 cm)
Photograph by Ruth Carey

and pieces of wood with interesting grains, for example—can also be pressed into the clay. Even the texture of a piece of cloth or plastic string-bag (Photo 43) can be impressed by placing the cloth or bag over your tile slab and then rolling over it.

Using this technique in combination with the colored slip inlay method, described on pages 64-66, will result in a beautiful and unique surface. Just impress your design and fill the recessed impression lines with slip.

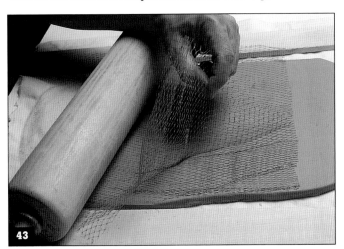

43

Underglazes

Underglazes, which may be applied to greenware or to bisque, are ceramic pigments in liquid form. They derive their name from the fact that they are often covered with glazes, which brighten their otherwise dull and matte colors, affix them to the tile, and provide a glasslike coating over them. Put simply, underglazes go under glazes.

The modified *metallic oxides* in underglazes give them their color. Cobalt oxides yield blue, for example, copper oxides yield green, and manganese oxides yield black. Underglazes can be mixed by hand, but because

the metallic oxides in them are toxic, beginners should work only with premixed commercial underglazes, available in 4-ounce (113.4 g) jars. When you purchase underglazes, which are relatively inexpensive, check the descriptions on the jars' labels to make sure that you get types that can be applied to either greenware or bisque.

As well as oxides, underglazes also contain a little *fluxing material*. During firing, the fluxing agent makes the underglaze melt just enough to hold it onto the clay but not enough to become sticky. Note that underglazes, because they don't melt into a glasslike state as glazes do, aren't waterproof, and unless they've been covered with a glaze, they can be rubbed off the tile, even after they've been fired.

Painting with Underglazes

Painting tiles with commercial underglazes is one of the most accessible forms of tile decoration. Though designs may be created with either underglazes or glazes, one advantage to using underglazes is that their colors, unlike those of glazes, usually look very much the same on the fired tile as they do in the bottle. (Note that underglaze colors will always be brighter after a clear glaze has been fired on top of them.) Composing underglaze colors in chromatic relationship to one another as you work is therefore relatively easy. In addition, underglaze colors do not run into one another on the tile as glaze colors do.

As with many other painting pigments, most underglazes of the same type can be blended together before application. Mixing some white with a medium-blue underglaze, for example, will result in a lighter blue. A plastic ice-cube tray makes an excellent underglaze mixing and painting pallet. Underglazes are water soluble; when they dry out in the tray, you can bring them back to working consistency by adding water.

When underglazes are applied to greenware, the clay should be in the latter stages of leatherhard or bone-dry. Working with greenware has one disadvantage. Unfired clay is brittle and fragile, while bisque, which is harder, is somewhat easier to handle. In spite of this fact, many tile makers prefer to apply underglazes to greenware. They feel that by doing so they can obtain a more opaque covering with fewer visible brush marks.

Another advantage to applying underglazes to unfired clay is that it often saves a firing step. Underglaze decoration on greenware is solidified and affixed to the tile by bisque firing. A clear glaze is then brushed onto the bisque-fired underglaze, and the tile is glaze fired. If you apply your underglaze to bisque, an intermediate firing may be necessary because the underglaze hasn't been affixed by heat; brushing glaze over an unfired underglaze may smear it. This is especially true when your work is very detailed. It would be best to either fire the underglaze before brushing on the glaze or apply the glaze by spraying or dipping.

Applying underglazes to unfired clay has one additional benefit. If you miss any spots as you paint or the underglaze leaves streaks, you'll be able to see them before they're sealed underneath a clear glaze. After the underglaze is bisqued onto the tile, wetting the tile with water to make its surface shiny will make any imperfections show up right away. You can then touch up the tile with extra underglaze. If you apply the underglaze to a bisque tile and then cover it with a glaze, you won't notice the bare spots and streaks and will be stuck with them after the glaze firing.

Note in Photo 44 that the bone-dry terra-cotta tile was first painted with a coat of white slip. This slip provides a bright background for underglaze colors. (For a full description of slips and their application, see the sections that follow.)

44

Once your design has been transferred to the surface of the clay (or to the coat of slip), use a brush of an appropriate width to paint your underglaze onto the tile. Always stir the underglaze before you use it and cap the bottle or cover the tray with plastic when it's not in use so that the underglaze won't dry out. For an opaque covering on greenware, three coats of underglaze are generally recommended. Allow each coat to dry before applying the next.

It's possible to effectively cover and obliterate one color by painting over it with another. It is also possible

Opposite page: Rodger Dunham
Untitled. 1991
45 sq. ft. (4.18 m²)
Photograph by Rodger Dunham

Left: Rodger Dunham
Untitled. 1991
60 sq. ft. (5.57 m²)
Photograph by Rodger Dunham

Top of page: Ginger Legato
Woman in Water. 1986
72" x 72" (182.9 x 182.9 cm)

Above: Joan Gardiner
Dolphin (from *Wave Border Design*). 1991
4" x 7-1/2" (10.2 x 19.1 cm)
Photograph by Sarah Huntington

Natalie Surving
Tree Frog with
Maple Leaf. 1991
Each 4" x 4" x 5/16"
(10.2 x 10.2 x .8 cm)

Affra Gibbs
Rosie. 1992
4-1/4" x 4-1/4"
(10.8 x 10.8 cm)
Photograph by Bobby Hansson

to create a light, transparent covering on your tile, similar to those in a watercolor painting, by thinning appropriate underglazes, but thinned underglazes should be applied only to bisque, not to greenware. An unfired tile's surface will become muddy from the amount of water necessary to achieve this effect.

Instead of painting your design with underglazes on greenware, it's also possible to paint the design with glaze colors on bisque (see chapter 9). Remember, however, that glaze colors will run into each other. If you're aiming for a bright, shiny glaze surface and a multicolored, sharp-edged design (one in which different colors don't blur where they touch each other), paint your design with underglazes, bisque fire the tile, and then follow with a low-fire, clear glaze coating. The tile maker who created the "baby" tile shown above has made excellent use of painted underglazes to provide a cheerful, playful look.

Spraying with Underglazes

For the most subtle shading and color application, underglaze colors can also be thinned and applied to greenware or to bisque with an airbrush. With practice and skill, the colors can be worked as effectively as on any airbrush painting. Note that these thinned underglazes won't cause the surface of the unglazed tile to become muddy; a sprayed underglaze mist won't pool on the tile as a thinned and brushed underglaze would. After air-brushing, bisque fire the tile and then brush on a clear glaze or apply that glaze with an airbrush.

A simpler way to achieve an air-brush effect is to spatter underglaze colors onto the unfired tile with a bristle brush or toothbrush. Try using a flat object (a leaf, for example) as a stencil. Place the object onto the tile and then run your gloved finger across the bristles of a brush that's been dipped into underglaze. Be sure to run your finger toward you so that the spray projects away from you and onto the tile. By doing this, it's possible to build up a pattern of silhouetted shapes on your tile and to create a soft, dotted color surface. The sprayed design will dry almost instantly. This technique,

probably familiar to you from childhood art projects, can yield quite sophisticated results when adult control and creativity are added.

If you've applied your underglaze to bone-dry ware, your tile can be bisque fired right away. If your tile was leatherhard, wait for it to become bone dry before firing it.

Slips and Engobes

You may hear the terms *slips* and *engobes* used interchangeably, but there is a technical difference between the two. Slips, which can be as thin as underglazes or as thick as cake icing, are clay in a liquid form, with or without added oxides or color pigments. Though slips for bisque are available, slips are usually applied to greenware at its early leatherhard stage.

Engobes are also liquid clay compositions. Unlike slips, however, they contain *frits* or other fluxing agents that make them melt when they're fired. Frits are pulverized, glasslike materials (also found in glazes), which give a slight sheen to engobes. Engobes do not melt down to a flat and glassy state as glazes do; they retain a raised, dryer surface. Glazes, which contain more frit, become much more vitreous during firing.

Note that underglazes are much like engobes but are usually thinner. Engobes can be modified to meet specific needs by varying the amount of each ingredient when they're mixed. Slips usually have more body and thickness than engobes and retain a more raised surface even after firing.

Engobes work best when they're applied to moist and leatherhard greenware. They're not usually applied to bisque, though by adjusting the amount of fluxing agent in an engobe formula, it is possible to formulate an engobe for fired tiles.

Because both slips and engobes contain a high percentage of clay, they must *fit* the clay bodies to which they are applied so that they dry, shrink, and fire at a rate similar to that of the tile. Unless they fit, they may crack or separate from the tile and fall off it. To determine if a proper fit has been achieved, test fire slips and engobes on the clay that you're using. (You may never

Above: Frank Giorgini
Butterfly. 1993
12" x 12" (30.5 x 30.5 cm)
Photograph by Bobby Hansson

Right: Vivika Heino
Bamboo Tile. 1988
30" x 18" (76.2 x 45.7 cm)
Photograph by Bill Dow

Below: Vivika Heino
Fern Leaves. 1993
14-1/2" x 16" (36.8 x 40.6 cm)
Photograph by Bill Dow

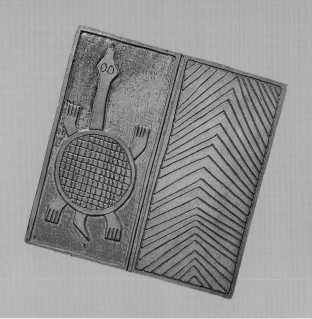

even get to the test-firing stage; if you apply a slip to a leatherhard or bone-dry tile, and it peels off as the tile dries, you'll know right away that there's a problem with the fit!) Because slips do not contain the fluxing agents that help to attach engobes to clay, their fit becomes especially important. They must go on unfired clay so that they can dry and shrink as the clay does.

Slips and engobes are available through many companies. Colored slips can also be formulated in the studio by adding various oxide stains to a base white slip. Even underglazes can be added to slips to obtain a variety of colors. Beginners should avoid mixing their own formulas, but for experienced ceramists, slip formulas are provided in Appendix C on page 138.

Both slips and engobes may be applied by painting or spraying. They can sometimes be applied by dipping on bisque tiles (see chapter 9). Neither slips nor engobes will run, but when you paint them onto your tile, be sure to let each coat dry before you apply the next.

Slip Trailing

The method that takes full advantage of a slip's fullbodied properties is *slip trailing*—the application of slip through a tube. This technique is most appropriate for clay in the early stages of leatherhard.

First fill a plastic dispenser bottle, one with a long,

narrow neck, with a slip of a color that contrasts with your moist clay tile. To create a raised surface of dots and lines, squeeze the thick liquid out onto the tile as if you were decorating a cake. Then cover up the tiles with plastic and dry them slowly.

The unfired stoneware tile shown in Photos 45 and 46 has first been painted with white slip. The design is being slip trailed over that base white coat.

Inlaid Tiles

In contrast to tiles decorated with underglazes, *inlaid* (or *encaustic*) tiles are decorated by embedding colored clays or clay slips into the surface of the tile. Because an inlaid design penetrates below the tile's surface, its colors do not wear away. For this reason, inlaid tiles have long been popular as floor coverings. Development of the encaustic method is usually attributed to twelfth-century Cistercian monks, who produced paving tiles for English monasteries.

The colored clay for inlay work is made by mixing powdered colorants such as stains and oxides with a light-colored clay base. This is a messy and unpleasant task, so try to purchase precolored moist clays, which are available in 25-pound (11.4 kg) bags from many clay supply houses. The colored clay, which should fit the clay body of your tile, is then rolled or pressed into

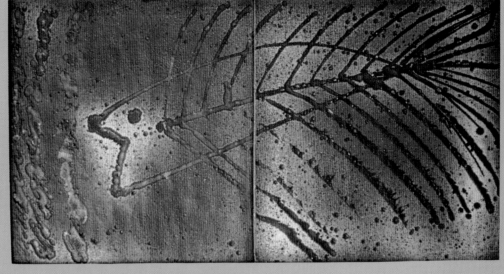

Opposite page, left: Bernadette Stillo
Lovers in the Grass. 1992
5-3/4" x 7-3/4" (14.6 x 19.7 cm)
Photograph by Bobby Hansson

Opposite page, right: Frank Giorgini
Afro Tile. 1993
12" x 12" (30.5 x 30.5 cm)
Photograph by Bobby Hansson

Right: Otto Heino
Fish Panel. 1984
14-1/2" x 16" (36.8 x 40.6 cm)

recessed design areas on the soft base tile.

One way to create an encaustic effect is to first roll out a clay slab that is the desired thickness of your tile. Then arrange the coils of colored clay on its surface and use a rolling pin to press the coils into the slab until the surface of the slab is level. You may also use a slab roller to do this pressing job for you.

When using clay slips with the inlay method, it's best to work on leatherhard tiles and to use fairly thick slips. First, incise your design with handmade incising tools or with a notched blade tool, similar to the one used in linoleum-block cutting (Photo 47). (See chapter 14 for instructions on making the former.)

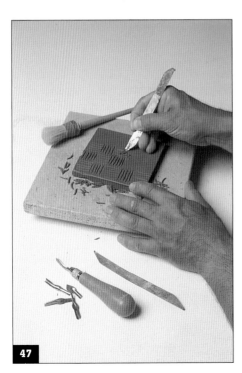

Next, fill in the recessed areas with clay slip. If your design lines are many, you may want to use a wide brush to coat the whole tile with slip first (Photo 48). When that coat of slip has dried slightly (in about fifteen

minutes), repeat the process until the slip has built up over the incised design.

If the incised design lines are shallow and few, just dab the slip into the grooves. Keep adding slip; the previous coat will shrink as it dries. Continue to apply the slip until it builds up in the areas over the incised design and protrudes above the original tile surface.

Let the tile and slip dry to the advanced leatherhard stage. Then use the edge of a metal rib to scrape off the excess slip (Photo 49) until you reach the uppermost

surface of the original tile (Photo 50). You'll achieve a cleaner finish if you scrape in the same direction as the inlaid slip or clay rather than scraping perpendicular to those lines.

50

Scraping the tile when the clay is still soft will smear its surface, but scraping a bone-dry tile will produce more clay dust than is good for your health. Scrape only when the tile is leatherhard. Be sure to wear a dust mask when you do this and to collect the scrapings for disposal.

Narrow incised lines don't usually provide problems. If your inlay design incorporates large recessed areas, however, two problems may occur. The slip in these areas may separate from the edges of the incised clay around it and may crack as the tile dries or is fired. Both problems result from the different shrinkage rates and moisture content of the slip and the clay body. Either stick with narrow incised lines, cross-hatching, and notching (the effect of shrinkage in these smaller areas is minimal), or engage in some extensive testing.

Once the tile has been bisque fired, you may wish to coat it with a clear glaze. Alternatively, if you'd rather that the surface of your tile not be shiny, be sure to fire the tile up to or close to its vitrification point in order to make it strong and water resistant.

Sgraffiato

Sgraffiato, another method of decoration for unfired tiles, makes use of either underglazes (applied to leatherhard or bone-dry tiles) or clay slip (applied to relatively moist tiles). In this technique, the tile is first painted with one or more layers of colored slips or underglazes. After the coats have dried, the design is cut or scraped through the layers with a pin tool, craft knife, or trimming tool to reveal the clay body underneath (Photo 51). Other tools can be used, of course; just experiment to find the one that's best suited to your design.

51

Underglazes, which are thinner than slips and which dry very quickly, are best for fine-lined sgraffiato

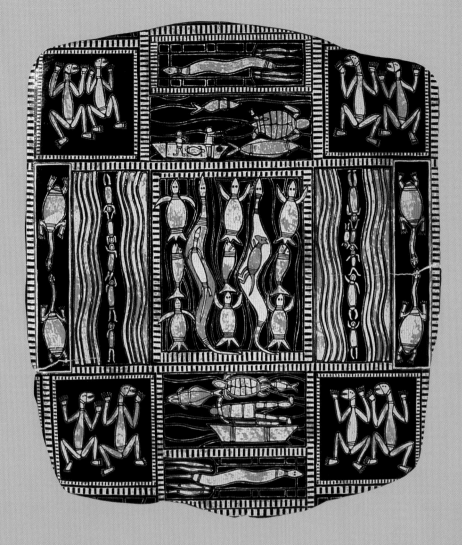

Lynda Curtis
Yirkalla. 1993
Image: 22-1/2" x 19" (57.2 x 48.3 cm)
Photograph by Bobby Hansson

Lynda Curtis
The Elephant Dance. 1992
Image: 4" x 12" (10.2 x 30.5 cm)
Photograph by Van Blerck Photography

Left: Tamara Jaeger
Super Woman. 1991
6" x 6" (15.2 x 15.2 cm)
Photograph by Chas Krider

Below: Cairo Cocalis
Reptile Jungle
Each 6" x 6" (15.2 x 15.2 cm)
Photograph by Elizabeth Vanderkooy

Paula Camenzind
Untitled. 1992
Each 15-1/2" x 6-1/2"
(39.4 x 16.5 cm)
Photograph by Carlos Alejandro

designs; clay slips tend to be too thick for use when designs are highly detailed. When using underglazes, apply two thin coats of each color. (Because underglazes dry quickly, you will probably be able to complete this task and transfer your design onto the tile in a single day.) Though underglazes do not need to be matched for fit, slips do.

For the boldest sgraffiato look, use only one color of slip or underglaze, a color that will contrast with the clay body once the design has been carved. For a more subtle but very beautiful effect, apply several layers of different colored slips. When you cut the design through the layered colors, the edge of each cut will offer a rainbow effect.

To transfer your design to the underglaze- or slip-covered surface, first place the tile on a turntable. Then rest the design paper (face up) on top of the tile, taping the paper to the table to keep it secure. Trace the design onto the tile by pressing firmly on the design lines with a pin tool or blunt pencil. The tool or pencil will mark the underglaze or slip underneath without piercing the paper. To transfer very simple designs, just use a pencil to draw the design directly onto the underglaze or slip.

Shellac Resist

Shellac resist is a technique borrowed from print making. The shellac is applied to specific design areas on an unfired tile, one with or without underglazes or slips on it. (Wax, polyurethane, or oil-based inks can also be used, though shellac seems to work best.) Once it has dried, the shellac acts as a waterproof resist, protecting the areas that it covers. The exposed areas of the tile are then etched away by gently rubbing the entire tile surface with a dampened sponge. Because the unprotected part of the tile's surface is eroded away and is rough in appearance, shellac-resist tiles tend to have a primitive look. This technique therefore lends itself to

designs of an organic nature and to ancient motifs.

Shellac can be purchased at a hardware store. Also buy some denatured alcohol with which to clean your brushes; neither turpentine nor water will work. If your tile has no slip or underglaze on it, make sure that the tile surface is smooth so that the finished tile will provide an interesting contrast between the textures of smooth and eroded areas. To remove the rolled-out canvas texture, run the flat side of your rubber rib over the tile while the clay is still moist.

Then transfer the design to your bone-dry or leatherhard tile. Next, in a well-ventilated work space or outdoors, paint the shellac onto the areas of your design that you'd like to protect. Shellac, incidentally, can be used right out of the can. In fact, as the alcohol in it evaporates, the shellac will get thicker and will be easier to apply. If it gets too thick, just thin it with some of the alcohol.

For best results, apply the shellac to a bone-dry tile or to one at the advanced leatherhard stage; the bone-dry stage is preferable. Shellac applied to a moist tile may buckle and peel off as the tile dries and shrinks. In addition, the shellac won't be absorbed as quickly by moist clay; painting thin lines will be difficult because the shellac will flow and spread.

After painting on your design, wait until the shellac is dry to the touch before you proceed. (Alcohol-based shellac actually dries quite quickly.) For even better results, allow the shellac to dry for a couple of hours or overnight. Then rub the entire tile surface gently with a damp sponge to erode the unprotected surface areas. (If you've applied the shellac to a bone-dry tile, you can sponge off the surface at any later date, but if the tile is leatherhard, complete the rubbing process shortly after the shellac dries.)

During the bisque firing, the shellac will burn away, leaving a surface of low, flat relief and strong contrasts between smooth and rough textures. All

Bobby Hansson
Donna Maria—Vamping.
1976
6" x 6" (15.2 x 15.2 cm)
Photograph by Bobby Hansson

Bobby Hansson
Carrie Nation. 1976
6" x 6"
(15.2 x 15.2 cm)
Photograph by Bobby Hansson

shellac-covered design areas will be smooth and the same height as the original tile surface. The areas that you've rubbed with the sponge will be recessed, and because the clay body's grog is now exposed, these eroded surfaces will also have a grainy, sand-like texture.

A variation on the basic technique is shown in Photos 52 and 53. First apply a coat of colored slip or underglaze slip to the entire tile surface and then let it

52

dry. On bone-dry ware, drying won't take long; on a leatherhard tile, it may take one or two hours. Then apply the shellac. After the tile is sponged, the areas that were protected by the shellac resist will be the color of the slip; they'll also be smooth and above the recessed, textured surface of the background clay body (see *Butterfly* tile on page 63).

You can also use oil-based printer's ink as a resist

by applying it through a screen as in screen printing (see the next section) and then wiping the design areas.

53

Screen Printing on Tiles

Screen printing, which can be done on either greenware or bisque, is a sophisticated method of stenciling and is a technique with two advantages for the tile maker. The technique makes it possible both to transfer an exact image (of either a sketch or a photograph) onto a tile and to print this exact image on tiles as many times as desired.

The basic procedure entails using a squeegee to pull an underglaze over the open areas of the screen, leaving an even deposit of underglaze on the tile. The tile can then be glazed or left unglazed. Whether you print on bisque or greenware, the tile must be fired after printing.

First, take your photograph or sketch to a copy shop and have the shop make a *separation* of it; this is a copy of the image that has been shot onto acetate. If your art work is black and white, with no gray tones or shadows, ask to have it shot as *line art*, which is generally easiest to print on tiles. Art work with gray tones and shadows, on the other hand, needs to be shot with *halftones*; these are the tiny dots that you see when you look at a newspaper photograph. In order to print easi-

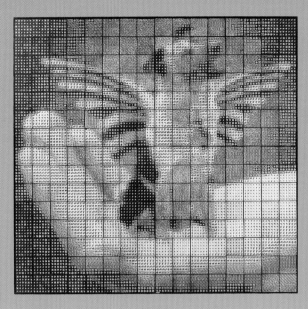

Robert Stratton and Sandra McLean
Detail of *Maya* (shown at right). 1992

Robert Stratton and Sandra McClean
Maya. 1992
69" x 72" (175.3 x 182.9 cm)

ly, the halftone dots have to be large. Ask the copy shop to shoot halftone images at thirty dots per inch (11.8 per cm). This is double the usual size for printing; the shop may need to blow up an intermediate negative to get dots this large. You, in turn, may have to insist that you know what you're talking about when you make this request—it's an unusual one!

It's also possible to make your own separation, using an opaque black pen or a black oil crayon, by drawing directly on "prepared" acetate, which can be purchased at any art supply store. Nuances obtained with the black oil crayons transfer quite well onto the screen.

Once you have your separation, bring it to your screen-printing supply store and ask them to shoot it onto the screen for you. If you have difficulty finding a copy shop to make a separation, the screen-printing store can do this, too.

At this point, you'll be ordering a screen and purchasing a squeegee. The squeegee should be 3" (7.6 cm) larger than your tile in each dimension and should also be at least 2" (5.1 cm) smaller than the inside dimensions of your screen. For a 4" x 4" (10.2 cm x 10.2 cm) tile, for example, you'll need a 7" (17.8 cm) squeegee.

Purchase a screen that's at least 8" (20.3 cm) larger in each dimension than the tile that you plan to print. For a 4" x 4" (10.2 cm x 10.2 cm) tile, buy a screen that is 12" x 12" (30.5 cm x 30.5 cm) or larger. The screen mesh should be fairly coarse (12XX, 14XX, or 16XX), especially if you're a beginner. The higher the mesh number, the finer the mesh will be. The finer the mesh, the more detailed the image, but dried underglaze will also clog finer screens more rapidly than coarse ones. Screens with smaller number sizes hold less detail but will deposit more underglaze.

The supply store will build the screen to your exact size and mesh specifications. To save money, get a screen that is large enough to have several images shot onto it. The cost of one large screen is significantly less than the cost of several small ones. A screen can be re-used many times; just ask the

supply store to put a new image on it.

If you have access to a studio where you can shoot the screen yourself, by all means do so. There are kits available for home shooting, but they're expensive, and we can't recommend them.

Printing on tiles should be executed with commercial underglazes. The consistency of your underglaze is very important; it should be about as thick as standard white glue. Underglaze that's used straight out of the jar is likely to be too thin; it will run underneath the stencil and cause the image to bleed. To thicken it, leave the jar lid off for a few hours. If it's too thick, it may clog the stencil, but too thick is better than too thin.

It's possible to print on both handmade and commercial tiles. Commercial tiles are certainly easier to handle because their surfaces tend to be perfectly flat. They're also uniform in size, which makes registration easier. Handmade tiles, on the other hand, are never perfectly flat or uniform in size; therein lies their beauty. If you do use tiles that you've made yourself, smooth them out as much as possible. The more detailed your image, the flatter your tile needs to be. Even the indentations left by the canvas will inhibit printing. To create a smooth surface, try sponge-brushing your tiles with slip. Line art is probably best for handmade tiles because halftone dots may not print well on tiles that aren't perfectly flat.

Two printing methods are possible. The simplest way to print is unfortunately somewhat inefficient; it necessitates cleaning the screen each time you print a tile. Rest the screen on strips of wood so that the fabric is positioned about 1/2" (1.3 cm) away from the tile. Then surround your tile with extra tiles; doing so will provide a smooth transition for your squeegee as it moves across and off the tile that you're printing.

Look through the screen, pushing down on it so that you can see better, and align the stencil (or image) with the tile. Have someone hold the screen frame firmly. Next, pour a bead of underglaze across the top of the screen, one slightly longer than the tile itself. Then pull the squeegee across the screen while pressing the screen against the tile (Photo 54). Do this just once, holding the squeegee at a 45° angle and maintaining firm and even pressure on it. As soon as you've made this single pass with the squeegee, the mesh will spring back away from the tile's surface. Lift the screen away carefully to see your printed tile (Photo 55). Clean the screen by running it under cold water and wiping it off with a sponge. Hold it up to the light and make sure that you can see through it.

The second printing method, simultaneously more complicated and more efficient, involves using pur-chased *screen clamps*, which serve to fasten one edge of the screen to a piece of plywood. The screen can then be swung up and down while you print several tiles—one after another—without shifting the screen's printing position. Before you use the clamped screen, register the exact position in which the tiles will be placed by drawing the tile shape onto your work sur-face. By placing each tile within this marked outline, you'll ensure that the screen is lowered into the same position on every tile. Several tiles can be printed before the screen will need to be cleaned.

The screen-printing process requires practice, so don't get discouraged. Save tiles by practicing on paper instead. Just cut some newsprint to the size of your actual tiles and place a sheet on top of a tile that's ready to print. Keep practicing on one sheet of newsprint after another, until you're ready to print on the actual tile. If you run into problems, the suggestions that follow may help to solve them.

Only parts of the image are printing:
  • The underglaze has dried on the screen. Wash the screen, dry it with a towel, and try again.
  • You don't have enough underglaze on the screen. Same solution as above.

  • You aren't applying enough pressure to the squeegee. Try again on a different tile.
  • The tile isn't flat. Select a flatter tile and try again.

A vertical line appears across the image on the tile:
  • Dried underglaze has stuck to the squeegee. Wash the squeegee and try again.
  • There may be a nick in the squeegee. Use the other side of the squeegee on a new tile.

The image is bleeding:
  • The underglaze is too thin. Let the underglaze thicken in the open air and try again on another tile.
  • You are holding the squeegee at too sharp an angle. Try again on another tile.

CHAPTER EIGHT

FIRING TO HARDNESS

Bonnie Johnson
She Wants to Learn to Dance. 1986
30.5" x 21" x 6" (77.5 x 53.3 x 15.2 cm)
Photograph by Steve duFour

Marcia Hovland
Untitled. 1993
Each 4" x 4" (10.2 x 10.2 cm)
Photograph by Denis DeSandre

Bisque Firing

Unfired, dried clay that is placed in water will disintegrate and turn back into moist clay. With the application of sufficient heat, however, your clay tile will undergo an irreversible chemical change (known as the *ceramic change*) and will turn into a stonelike material that is no longer water soluble.

Bisque firing, the first firing that your tile will undergo, hardens the tile and makes it easier to handle when you glaze it. It also allows gases in the clay to escape before the clay is covered with an impervious glaze. If your tile warps or cracks during the bisque firing, you needn't bother to glaze it and fire it again; just discard it.

There will always be some chemically-bound moisture in your unfired tiles—moisture that's related to atmospheric humidity and pressure—but the tiles must be bone dry before they're loaded into the kiln. If the tile is fired before most of this moisture has had a chance to evaporate, the moisture will turn to steam, and as it tries to escape, will cause the tile to crack or explode.

A standard bisque-firing temperature, no matter what kind of clay you're using, is about cone 06 to cone 04 but may be lower or higher to accommodate particular glazing techniques. If, for instance, you wanted an especially strong tile with a low-fire glaze, you might bisque fire the tile at cone 2—a higher temperature than standard—for strength, and then fire the glaze at a temperature that would actually be lower than the bisque-firing temperature. Different temperatures affect the application of glazes onto your tiles.

Don't bisque fire at temperatures that are too high. As a clay approaches final vitrification, it gets less and less porous, and glazes won't adhere to nonporous surfaces. Don't fire at too low a temperature (below cone 015) either, or the firing won't burn out all the carbon in the clay.

The Stages of Firing

A general knowledge of the physical and chemical changes that clay goes through during the firing process will help you to attain more successful firings.

The first stage of the slow heating that is required during bisque firing is called *water smoking* and may take one to several hours depending on the amount of moisture in the tiles, the size and thickness of each tile, and the number of tiles in the kiln. If all the moisture has not escaped by the time the temperature in the kiln has reached 100°C (212°F), then that moisture will turn to steam, which in turn may cause the clay to pop or shatter. For this reason, it's important to keep the firing temperatures from rising too rapidly at this stage; the steam must have time to escape.

As the temperature gradually rises to about 200°C (392°F), any vegetable matter in the clay breaks down and then decomposes. At 573°C (1063°F), an actual chemical change called *quartz inversion* takes place. At this stage, the clay becomes irreversibly hard.

From about 700°C to 900°C (1292°F to 1652°F), the clay's carbon and sulphur burn away and escape as gas. If you heat your tiles too quickly, the clay pores will start to close before these gases escape, and the gases will either form bubbles under the clay's nonporous surface or will cause the tile to bloat during subsequent firings. At this temperature range, if you look through the peepholes in the kiln, you'll see that the kiln's interior is a dull red. Bloating may not be apparent in the bisque but may appear during the glaze firing as the trapped carbon tries to escape. This carbon will appear as a dark core on the inside of a broken piece of bisque ware. Once all the carbon is gone, bisque firing is complete; the bisqued tile is irreversibly hard.

Vitrification, the final stage of firing clay to maturity, is the stage at which the clay becomes completely non-

Geoffrey Meek
Babylonian Lion of the Great Processional Way. 1987
43" x 103" (109.2 x 261.6 cm)

porous and glasslike—the point just before the clay loses structure and starts to melt. The temperature at which this stage starts can vary greatly with different clay bodies but usually begins around 800°C (1472°F). If a given clay is fired to a temperature higher than that required for vitrification, the clay will deform and melt into a glasslike state.

Kiln temperatures during bisque firing should not rise to those required for vitrification because the clay becomes less porous as the body becomes glassier. Clay fired to the bisque stage is still porous enough to allow liquid glaze to seep in and adhere to the surface of the tile. The subsequent glaze firing (see chapter 10) will bond the glaze to the clay, forming a waterproof, protective coating for your tiles.

Bisque-Firing Schedule

The typical firing schedule that follows, for a cone 06 to cone 04 bisque firing in either a 7 cu. ft. (.196 cu. meter) electric kiln or a .6 cu. ft. (.017 cu. meter) electric

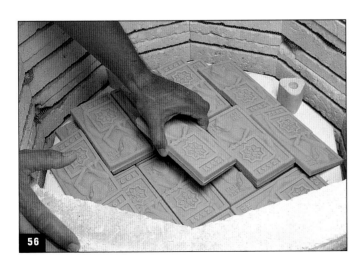

test kiln, will give you a rough idea of how bisque firing proceeds, but keep in mind that kilns vary widely. Follow the manufacturer's instructions carefully.

First, load your bone-dry tiles into the kiln, utilizing the available kiln furniture and space as efficiently as possible. By staggering the shelves in a way that permits the heat to circulate, it's possible to compensate for uneven heating within the kiln.

Small and medium-sized tiles, even ones that have been decorated with underglazes, can usually be stacked or leaned vertically against each other (Photo 56) for bisque firing. Underglazes don't become sticky during firing and won't cause the tiles to stick together.

Following are some suggested stacking heights for tiles of different sizes.

4" x 4" x 1/4" (10.2 cm x 10.2 cm x .6 cm)	Three to four tiles high
6" x 6" x 1/2" (15.2 cm x 15.2 cm x 1.3 cm)	Two to three tiles high
12" x 12" x 3/4" to 1" (30.5 cm x 30.5 cm x 1.9 cm to 2.5 cm))	Rest tiles flat on shelves

Unless they are well-supported on flat surfaces, tiles made with certain clays—those with lower vitrification points—may *slump* (or bend) during the bisque-firing process. Big, thick tiles, even those made with stoneware clays should be also be supported on a level surface. Sprinkling some grog on the shelf under a large tile will help it to shrink without stress.

As you arrange your kiln furniture, leave space between the shelves to allow the heat to circulate; about 3" to 4" (7.6 cm to 10.2 cm) over larger, thicker tiles will do.

Because the backs of stacked tiles aren't exposed to as much airflow as their sides, bloating can be a problem when you fire tiles. If you're accustomed to

Karen Koblitz
Bienveneda Still Life. 1988
36" x 60" x 7" (91.4 x 152.4 x 17.8)
Photograph by Susan Einstein

firing free-standing pottery, you'll need to slow down your firing schedule during the burning-out stage in order to compensate for the different way in which tiles are arranged in a kiln.

Insert the correct pyrometric cone into the kiln-sitter mechanism, selecting the cone to match the firing range you've chosen. For a standard bisque firing, you might use a cone 05. Keep in mind that the actual temperature in the kiln will often be one cone lower than the cone placed in the sitter.

It's always a good idea to place cone packs in several locations inside the kiln to indicate the actual temperature in each area. Though you won't be able to see all these packs through the peepholes, studying the cones after the firing is through will reveal the temperatures that were reached at those locations.

Cone packs are made from the same clay as your tiles and should contain some grog. Each pack also has holes pierced through it. The grog and holes will prevent the pack from exploding during the firing. Form a bowl-like depression in your cone pack to catch the melting cone material before it can drip onto your tiles.

Stick three cones into each pack, placing each cone at a slight angle. The first cone should be one that will bend at the lower end of the firing range to which you plan to fire your clay tile—cone 06 for a standard bisque firing. The middle cone—cone 05, for example—should reflect the temperature to which you want to fire your tile. And the final cone should be at the upper end of the firing range—cone 04. The kiln will be turned off when the middle cone in the pack has bent over. At that point, the first cone to have melted will probably be completely flat, and the remaining cone will still be upright.

Once the cone packs are in place, set the timer on the kiln for about twelve to thirteen hours and set the temperature control on low for two hours. Different kilns will have different temperature-control arrangements;

be sure to read and follow the manufacturer's instructions. Small electric kilns may have only two heating coils, one at the top and one at the bottom, with a switch that turns on one or both. Larger kilns, on the other hand, may have three or more separate dials, each of which controls a section of the kiln's interior.

Open all the peepholes in the kiln, and unless your kiln has a built-in arm for this purpose, use a brick or piece of kiln furniture to prop the lid open about 2" (5.1 cm). Cracking the lid during the early stages of firing will keep the kiln from heating too quickly and will allow the moisture and gases to escape.

After firing the kiln at low for two hours, set the temperature control at medium and continue the firing for another two hours.

Then turn the temperature control to high. If you're using a small electric test kiln, leave the one peephole in it open, but on larger kilns, close the peepholes at the bottom. Close the kiln lid and readjust the timer for about six to eight hours.

Either the kiln sitter (if the kiln has one) or the automatic timer will shut off the kiln—whichever mechanism is activated first. (The kiln will shut off automatically when the cone in the sitter melts. The automatic timer shuts off the kiln when the time runs out.) Keep an eye on the cone pack. If the cone 05 in it melts before the kiln shuts off automatically, turn the kiln off manually.

Before opening the door or closed peepholes, allow your tiles to cool in the kiln for at least ten hours. The flat planes of tiles are not as structurally sound as the curved spheres of fired pottery, so tiles are more susceptible to cracking from thermal shock. After ten hours have passed, you may open the peepholes and crack the lid open 2" (5.1 cm), but don't open the lid completely or remove the tiles for another two to three hours. Take out the tiles once they're cool to the touch.

CHAPTER NINE

SURFACE DECORATION
ON BISQUED TILES

Kenneth Dierck
Starry Night. 1992
15" x 15" x 1/4" (38.1 x 38.1 x .6 cm)
Photograph by John Eiselein

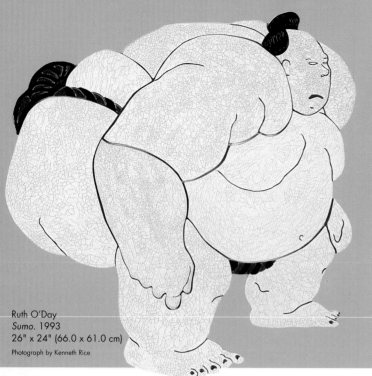

Ruth O'Day
Sumo. 1993
26" x 24" (66.0 x 61.0 cm)
Photograph by Kenneth Rice

Frank Giorgini
Lizard. 1991
6" x 6" (15.2 x 15.2 cm)
Photograph by Bobby Hansson

Glazes

Glazes, which contain more fluxing material than underglazes, melt and fuse onto the surface of a tile when the tile is fired, providing a hygienic, nonporous, waterproof coating that can be clear or colorful, shiny or matte, smooth or textured. Unlike underglazes, they actually seep into the tile and form a glasslike bond right down to the clay itself. As a general rule, glazes are not applied to greenware.

Available from your clay supplier, glazes come in 4-ounce to 16-ounce (113.4 g to 453.6 g) jars, in a wide palette of colors. In contrast to underglazes, however, their colors in the bottle often have no relationship to their fired colors. This can make application a mystery. Your supplier is likely to have a glaze-color guide consisting of glazed and fired clay buttons. You'll find this guide very helpful when you select glaze colors.

Glazes can be formulated from dry, powdered ingredients—clays, frits, oxides, and others—but the process is health-hazardous and is not recommended for beginners. (For experts, some glaze formulas can be found in Appendix D on page 138.) Besides being potentially dangerous, glaze formulation requires the use of specialized equipment and working conditions. To learn about glaze chemistry, a science in itself, enroll in a local clay course where you'll have access both to the chemicals and to a safe working environment.

Firing cone 06 to cone 04 commercial glazes in an electric kiln is usually the most accessible method available for glaze firing. Other methods of glaze firing, including stoneware, reduction, raku, salt, and saggar, require equipment and techniques too specialized for inclusion in this book, but brief descriptions of each are given in the next chapter.

As your work progresses, you'll no doubt wish to experiment with more unique glaze surfaces than are yielded by commercially available glazes, as well as with different firing techniques. Using premixed commercial glazes, however, is definitely the easier way to start.

It's not uncommon to work long and hard to create a unique hand-pressed relief tile, only to have it look gaudy and cheap because of an inappropriate commercial glaze choice. Your selection of glazes will depend upon a number of factors; understanding these will help you to make wise choices.

As explained in chapter 2, the kiln that you'll be using may limit your choice of glazes. Some glazes are made for oxidation firing; others must be reduction fired. Certain stoneware glazes, which require firing temperatures up to cone 10, just won't work in a small electric kiln.

Another factor that will influence your choice of glaze will be what you want your tile to look like. In general, shiny, colorful results are associated with low-fire glazes or with low-fire underglazes covered with a clear glaze. For earthy colors, with a mottled, breaking effect, choose higher temperature stoneware colors such as those in my *Lizard* tile (shown above).

As you gain experience with glazes, you will develop your own glaze-application techniques, as well as preferences for certain manufacturers' brands of glaze colors.

The most common methods of glaze application on bisque are brushing, dipping, and spraying, though spraying is usually done with underglazes instead. Glazes, like underglazes, can be thinned with water to the proper consistency for each method. Stir your glaze before you use it, as some ingredients tend to settle to the bottom. If the glaze has dried out, just add water before stirring. Also make sure that your tile is free of dust and oils; rinse it in water and let it dry until the little puddles of water on the surface disappear.

Kenneth Dierck
Bird Watcher. 1991
31" x 30-1/2" x 5/8" (78.7 x 77.5 x 1.6 cm)
Photograph by John Eiselein

Susan Grossman
Untitled. 1991
6" x 6" (15.2 x 15.2 cm)
Photograph by Susan Grossman

Painting with Glazes

Designs that are painted with glazes will yield entirely different results from those that are painted with underglazes. Commercial low-fire glazes on a bisque surface will produce bright colors, but the edges where two colors meet will flow and meld together during the subsequent glaze firing. Of course, you may be aiming for this effect.

To paint with glazes, use soft brushes in sizes compatible with your design. Most commercial glazes are applied in two or three even coats, and time is allowed for each coat to dry before the next is applied. Do check instructions on the glaze container before you start, but feel free to experiment by mixing colors, too. Keep in mind that the edges where two colors touch or overlap will form a third blended color.

Majolica glaze is especially versatile. Now formulated without tin because of the dangers of metallic oxides, majolica is a low-fire glaze and is usually a creamy, translucent white. It makes a good base glaze over which colored stains and oxides can be brushed. The stains and oxides sink and blend into the glaze surface during the glaze firing, providing a painted effect. Majolica can also be applied with other glazes or applied under or over underglazes.

No matter which glaze application technique you choose, you must be sure not to apply glaze to the back surface of your tile. If you're brushing the glaze on, cover only the top surface and leave an unglazed area about 1/8" to 1/4" (.3 cm to .6 cm) wide along the bottom of the tile's edge. Glaze that completely covers the edges or that covers the bottom will melt in the firing and will fuse your tile right onto the kiln shelf. To remove the tile—a very unpleasant task—you'd have to use a hammer, chisel, and grinder.

Wax Resist for Glaze Separation

To keep glaze colors from blending into one another in fine-lined designs, try the *wax-resist* technique. In this technique, a fine line of wax resist is painted between the design areas before glaze colors are applied. The wax burns off in the firing, leaving a narrow, dry area of bare tile visible between the glaze colors. This is a variation of a traditional resist technique called *cuerda seca* (see page 10) and is very effective with terra-cotta tiles; the warm terra-cotta color that appears between the glaze colors is especially attractive.

By mixing oxides with the wax resist, it's possible to apply colors to the dry lines between glazes, too. When the wax burns away, the oxide color will remain on the tile.

A similar, cloisonné effect can be created on tiles pressed out with carved plaster blocks by applying glaze colors between the raised design areas. These raised areas will prevent the colors from blending with each other. Unless you paint these surfaces with an underglaze first, they'll remain the color of your clay.

Dipping with Glazes

Dipping bisqued tiles into glazes is an application process that produces a very uniform coating. (You wouldn't usually dip greenware into an underglaze; an unfired tile might become muddy if it were dipped, and the process would require more underglaze than you're likely to have on hand.)

Before the tile is dipped, its entire back surface and the bottom portion of its edges must be covered with a wax resist so that the glaze will stick only to the front of the tile. A water-based wax resist is commercially available and is safer to use than hot paraffin. Inexpensive foam brushes make excellent applicators for the wax. Either hold the tile in one hand while you brush on the

Above: Barbara Grygutis
American Loveseat. 1993
Kenneth Myer Park,
Coconut Grove, Florida
36" x 72" x 72"
(91.4 x 182.9 x 182.9)
Photograph by Barbara Grygutis

Left: Barbara Grygutis
Cruising San Mateo I. 1991
City of Albuquerque
Public Art Collection
264" x 192" x 72"
(670.6 x 487.7 x 182.9 cm)
Photograph by Tim Fuller

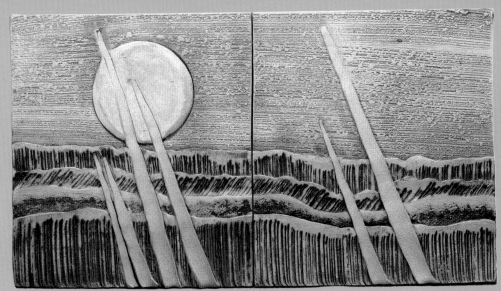

Daniel Oberti
Maquette. 1990
12" x 26" (30.5 x 66.0 cm)
Photograph by Daniel Oberti

wax with the other (Photo 57), or use a *tile-waxing stand* to hold the tile while the wax is applied (Photo 58). Instructions for making the tile-waxing stand are given in chapter 14.

Let the wax dry thoroughly. Have on hand enough glaze to cover the tile completely once the tile is submerged. The most efficient container for your glaze is a tall, narrow, or even rectangular bucket that's just wide enough to accommodate the tile.

A *tile dipper* will keep you from getting finger or clamp marks on the tile (Photo 59). See chapter 14 for instructions on how to make one of these useful tools from a wire coat-hanger or scrap wood. Position your tile so that it rests flat on the long arms of the tool and is supported along its bottom edge by the 90° wire ends. Hold the V-shaped end of the tool in your hand while you hold the tile down with your thumb. Submerge the tile completely in the glaze bucket. You shouldn't get

58

59

57

more than the tip of your gloved thumb wet during this process. Because the tile's back is covered with wax, no clamp or finger marks will be left on its surface.

Frank Giorgini
Elephant. 1992.
12" x 12" (30.5 x 30.5 cm)

Photograph Bobby Hansson

Pewabic Pottery
Fireplace Surround. 1988. 51" x 88" x 12" (129.5 x 223.5 x 30.5 cm)

Photograph by Tim Thayer

Lift the tile out of the dip (Photo 60) and shake it slightly to remove some of the excess glaze. Then place the tile (face up) on some newspaper. The glaze will be dry to the touch within half an hour, but make sure that its top surface is totally dry because you will have to handle it.

60

When the glaze is dry, gently hold the tile upside down with the glazed surface in the palm of your hand and use a damp sponge to remove any beads of glaze from the back. Don't handle the tile any more than necessary at this stage; the unfired glaze may wear off. If this should happen, just dab on a little more with a paintbrush.

The dipping technique works very well with relief tiles. By using a glaze that breaks into different colors as it flows and pools in the different areas of your design, you'll be able to achieve some spectacular results with a single dipping. The finished appearance of these types of breaking glazes can vary greatly depending upon the thickness of the application. The glaze coloration will look very natural because you've

allowed the breaking qualities of the glaze and the effects of the firing process to do the work for you.

One way to produce glazed areas that vary in thickness is to pour or dip additional glaze over the tile. Wait for the first coat to dry. Then hold or brace the tile inside a container (Photo 61). Scoop up some glaze with a smaller container and pour it over the front of the tile. The glaze will be thicker wherever the poured application overlaps. With certain glazes, the overlapped areas will also vary in color on the fired tile.

61

Glaze Scraping

An effective technique used in conjunction with dipping or pouring is to scrape the glaze off certain areas of your design, but unless you're working in a professional studio with excellent ventilation, this method should only be executed outdoors. It works best on tiles with raised, uniformly flat areas, such as those created with the layering technique. The *Elephant* tile shown above was made with this technique.

Dip or pour glaze over the entire front of the tile and let the glaze dry. (It will be workable within half an hour,

Karen Koblitz
Raffaellesco Deruta Lunette. 1993
23" x 41-1/2" x 7"
(58.4 x 105.4 x 17.8 cm)
Susan Einstein

but the tile can stand overnight if you like.) Spread out some newspaper on a table, place a turntable on top of the newspaper, and place the tile on top of the turntable. Be sure to put on a dust mask. Then, using a metal rib, scrape off most of the glaze on the raised areas of the tile (Photo 62). Whenever possible, scrape in the direction of the design lines, not perpendicular to them. Spin the turntable for easier access to these lines.

63

62

Next, rub a synthetic scouring pad over the scraped surfaces (Photo 63). Tip and shake the scrapings off the tile onto the newspaper. Don't blow the dust off; gently remove it with a soft brush instead. The finished tile will be glazed in the recessed areas, and the natural color of the clay will show through wherever you have scraped the glaze away.

A similar effect can be achieved by scraping the tile first and then using a damp sponge instead of a scouring pad. The sponge will pull some of the diluted glaze material across the clay and will leave the clay surfaces a bit shinier and darker than glazed clay that has been scraped and scoured. Using a sponge is also a much less dusty, and therefore safer, process.

Spraying with Glazes

Spraying is an efficient way to apply a uniform coating of glaze to your tile. It's also a good way to apply a clear glaze over underglazes painted onto bisque without smearing the unfired underglaze colors. This technique, however, requires a ventilated spray booth, a proper mask, and spray-gun equipment. In addition, practice is required to prepare glaze of the correct consistency, to adjust the spray pattern and pressure, and to gauge the correct distance from which to spray the tile. It is possible, however, to obtain fine results with sprayed underglazes or glazes—results that are comparable to delicate airbrush work with paints.

Note that it's difficult to apply an even coat of sprayed glaze over a relief tile, because the flow of spray over the uneven surface will often leave bare spots. Spraying over stencils on bisque ware is no different from spraying underglazes over stencils on greenware. When you use a stencil, glazes can also be patted on with a sponge or painted on with a brush.

Joseph A. Triplo
Study for Tile Floor. 1989
33" x 53" (83.8 x 134.6 cm)
Photograph by Dave Palmer

Stains

Stains are a mixture of water and coloring oxides, the natural materials from which the colors for glazes and underglazes are derived, and can be rubbed, brushed, sponged, or sprayed onto bisque. They're often applied to accent, recessed, or textured areas; the excess stain is rubbed off with a damp sponge to give an antique effect.

Stains will color clay whether or not it is glazed and will also affect glazes. They can be used at all firing ranges but their effects are greater at higher temperatures and in reduction firings. Following is a list of some oxides and their general color effects:

Chromium Oxide ....Green
Cobalt Carbonate........Blue
Copper Carbonate ......Warm Grey/Brown to Green
Iron Oxide ....Reddish Brown to Black
Manganese...................Black

Beginners should not attempt to mix their own stains as the ingredients can be toxic. Experienced tile makers mix stains in small batches by stirring a couple of teaspoons of oxide into a pint (473 ml) of water to make a thin, watery solution. Stain colorants, which come in a full range of colors, are available commercially in micronized crystal form (colored powders).

Underglazes on Bisque

Underglazes may be brushed or sprayed onto bisque, or sponged on and then off for an antique effect, but remember that your tile may require an additional firing before you coat the underglaze with a glaze, in order to prevent the underglaze colors from smearing. Commercial underglazes for painting are available in a set that resembles a child's watercolor set.

For a marbled effect on bisque, swirl together two or more underglaze colors in a shallow cookie sheet. Then press your bisque tile (face down) into the mixed colors. Pick up the tile, let it dry, fire it again, apply a clear glaze coating, and finally, glaze fire the marbled tile.

CHAPTER TEN

GLAZE FIRING, OVERGLAZES, AND DECALS

Anne Lloyd
Birches. 1993
8" x 5-1/2" (20.3 x 14.5 cm)
Photograph by John Carlano

Glaze-Firing Techniques

During the glaze firing, which is usually the second firing of your tile, the liquid glazes will fuse onto the tile's surface to provide a hygienic, waterproof, protective coating. While underglazes, which consist of clay slip and a small amount of fluxing material, will stick to the tile during bisque firing, glazes actually melt and fuse with the clay to form a glasslike coating. Note that glaze firing to a given temperature usually proceeds more rapidly than bisque firing to the same temperature because the chemical changes in the clay have already taken place.

A great many glaze-firing techniques have been perfected over the centuries. The source of heat (electric, gas, or solid-fuel kilns), the temperature range of the clay (low-fire earthenware or high-fire stoneware, for example), and the firing method (oxidation, reduction, raku, saggar, or salt), all yield an endless variety of surface finishes. Brief descriptions of these firing techniques follow, but the most accessible method is probably oxidation firing in an electric kiln. Try the library, a bookstore, or a ceramic supply house for further information on firing methods other than oxidation.

In *raku* firing, a technique that originated in sixteenth-century Japan, glazed or unglazed bisque or greenware is heated and rapidly cooled. Traditional Japanese tea bowls produced in this manner are extremely heat resistant and can be comfortably held even when their contents are very hot.

Today, the raku technique is used on all types of ceramic objects. Raku kilns, which are often gas fired, are usually located outdoors. The fired ware is removed from the kiln while it's still glowing hot and is placed in a container filled with combustible materials such as leaves, straw, newspaper, or sawdust. These materials are ignited by the heat of the ware, and the clay is blackened by the carbon in the heavy smoke that results. Raku-fired glazes often *crackle* (or *craze*); the thermal shock of the ware's rapid cooling creates beautiful, fine-lined cracks in the glaze, which are sometimes blackened by the carbon produced in this firing technique. Natural lusters often occur on raku glazes.

In *saggar* firing, the ware is placed in a lidded, refractory clay container filled with sawdust or other combustible materials. By creating this small, controlled atmosphere within the kiln, it's possible to affect the clay and the glazes in particular ways. The box also protects the ware from flames or gases. Saggar firing, like raku firing, may create smoke marks on the ware.

Salt firing, originally a German technique, is one in which the glaze is actually created during the firing. By introducing common salt into the kiln fire at certain intervals, soda is produced, which in turn combines with alumina and silica in the clay body to form a glaze on the ware's surface.

Glaze Firing

Because your tiles have been bisqued, they've already undergone the firing stages of water smoking, vegetable matter decomposition, ceramic change, and carbon and sulphur oxidation. For this reason, the general schedule of temperature rise in a glaze firing is somewhat different.

In the kiln, a slow drying period of low heat will remove any extra moisture in the glaze. The kiln temperature should rise gradually and steadily. At about 573°C (1063°F), a sudden expansion of the bisqued ware takes place, one that's a result of the crystalline silica structure of the clay. The point at which this expansion occurs is called the dunting point, and if the heat rise is rapid during this stage, stress cracks can occur in the tiles.

Up to the original temperature to which you bisque-fired your tiles, the clay body is unaffected. As the temperature rises and the glaze actually starts to melt, the clay body fuses with the glaze. This fusion (or integration) is what forms a strong glaze layer. At this stage, the glaze melts to glass and adheres permanently to the tile.

Anne Lloyd
Old-Time Baseball Player. 1993
14" x 6" (35.6 x 15.2 cm)
Photograph by John Carlano

Carol Susan Clemens
Burned Out. 1988
18" x 24" (45.7 x 61.0 cm)

Frank Giorgini
Afro Tile. 1992
12" x 12" (30.5 x 30.5 cm)
Photograph by Bobby Hansson

Opposite page: Penny Truitt
Outliers II. 1992
18" x 40" (45.7 x 101.6 cm)
Photograph by John Scarlata

If you've used the correct cone in the kiln sitter, the kiln should automatically shut off at this glaze maturation point. A back-up safety timer mechanism that will prevent overfiring is available for most kilns; be sure to get one.

Glaze-Firing Schedule

Always follow the kiln manufacturer's instructions for firing. To give you an idea of how a typical glaze firing might proceed, a firing schedule for a low-temperature glaze firing (cone 06 to cone 04) follows. This schedule is for a 7 cu. ft. (.196 cu. meter) electric kiln or a .6 cu. ft. (.017 cu. meter) electric test kiln. For a general high-temperature glaze-firing schedule in a gas kiln, see Appendix E on page 139.

When you load your tiles for a glaze firing, be sure that the backs of the tiles are free of glaze, that the glaze on the tiles is dry, and that the tiles don't touch each other (Photo 64). In its molten state, the glaze will flux and flow and stick to anything that it touches. Try to pack your kiln efficiently, using all available space.

64

Insert a cone 05 or cone 04 in the kiln sitter and set the timer for about ten hours. Then set the temperature control on low for one hour. Leave all the peepholes open and prop the lid up about 2" (5.1 cm), as shown in Photo 65.

65

When the hour has passed, reset the temperature control at medium for another hour, leaving the peepholes and lid as they were.

After that hour has passed, close the lid and all the peepholes except the top one. Set the temperature control at high and readjust the timer for about seven to eight hours. Depending upon the volume of tiles within the kiln, it will continue to fire for seven to eight hours.

After the kiln sitter has shut the kiln off, let the kiln cool for at least twelve hours. This cooling-down period, a very important stage of the glaze-firing process, is the period during which the colors of many glazes are set, and it may take twice as long as the actual firing. The kiln should be left closed so that it will cool naturally. If it

Opposite page:
John Bade
Wave. 1984
48" x 96" x 3/4"
(121.9 x 243.8
x 1.9 cm)
Photograph by Paul Kodama

Right: Frank Giorgini
Sunset mural from
fireplace and mural
installation. 1991
30" x 48"
(76.2 x 121.9 cm)
Photograph by Tom Teich

cools too rapidly, the glazes may craze, or the tile itself may crack. Note that if you'd like to create crazing on decorative ware, a commercial, clear crackle glaze is available, one that is formulated to crackle during normal cooling in an electric oxidation firing. By applying ink or stain over the cracks, you can create a look similar to raku. When the kiln is sufficiently cool to the touch, open the lid about 2" (5.1 cm).

When the interior has cooled completely, open the lid fully for a first look at your work. Opening a kiln is something like getting a present. Sometimes that present is wonderful—even spectacular—and the experience is exhilarating. At other times, you may wish you could return the gift for something else, but that's the excitement of working in ceramics.

Try to base your initial judgement of your finished tile on its own merits rather than on your expectations. If you don't like what you see, don't refire your tiles right away. Wait a day or two and take another look. You may very well find that your opinion has changed.

After removing your tiles from the kiln, don't stack them on top of one another without providing a cushioning layer of newspaper or cardboard between the layers.

Overglazes

Overglazes—very low temperature glazes that are applied to previously fired glazed surfaces—consist of coloring oxides and frits, usually in an oil medium. Similar to oil paints in consistency, they are brushed on and are fused onto the glazed surface in a separate cone 021 to cone 014 firing. This low firing range melts and fuses the overglazes without melting the previously fired glaze.

Commercially available from your ceramic supplier in a wide range of colors, overglazes are reasonably permanent but are not as durable as higher fired glazes. They do wear off with repeated rubbing and cleaning. Opaque colors are often referred to as *overglaze enamels* and transparent colors as *china paints*. Metallic overglazes, such as gold, silver, platinum, and copper are also available. These are quite expensive and are most commonly seen as gold or silver banding on tableware.

A thin metallic film of overglaze that covers the surface of a glaze is referred to as a *luster*. This thin metallic-oxide coating can be applied to the glazed ware by brush or as a spray, or can be produced on the glazed surface during the firing process through a technique called *fuming*. The result is lusterlike and iridescent.

Decorating with overglazes and lusters should only be undertaken with the greatest of care. Toxic chemicals can be released during both the application and firing processes, so proper masks and ventilation are a must. For health reasons, I do not use lusters and overglazes in the classroom environment.

Decals

Overglaze designs can also be applied in the form of printed decals. These are transferred by wetting a paper backing material and sliding the image off onto the fired glaze surface of your tile. The tile is then refired to cone 021 to 014 range. Decals may be ordered from certain silk-screening companies' catalogues, which contain hundreds of pre-made images. Black or (much more expensive) full-color decals can also be made up from your own designs or photographs. Cost is relative to the size of the decal, its colors, and the quantity desired. Be prepared to provide the decal printing company with camera-ready art work. Decals can be handmade, too, by screen printing them onto special decal paper.

Left: Susan Nowogrodzki
The Life Cycle: Water. 1987-1988
55" x 38" (139.7 x 96.5 cm)
Photograph by Neil McGreevy

Lower left: Wickie Lynn Bowman
Cow Skull. 1992
12" x 12" (30.5 x 30.5 cm)
Photograph by Julie Hicks

Below: Penny Truitt
Winter Beach II. 1990
18" x 22" (45.7 x 55.9 cm)
Photograph by John Scarlata

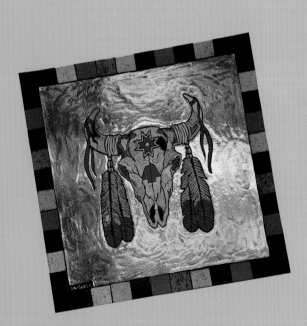

MOSAICS

Zuthbeida Lazrek
Mala Madre (Spider Plant). 1986
48" x 36" (121.9 x 91.4 cm)
Photograph by Z. Quiles

Diane Winters
Springfield Garden (detail). 1991
22" x 28" (55.9 x 71.1 cm)

Mosaic Materials and Composition

A *mosaic* is made by arranging pieces of durable materials to compose a permanent design. These materials are sometimes referred to as *tesserae* and include shaped tiles, broken pieces of tile, glass, and marble. The pieces can be set in cement (a process known as a *mud job*) or affixed to a solid surface with ceramic adhesives. *Grout*, a cementlike material, is used to fill the spaces between the installed tiles.

Mosaic Design

Basically, there are two ways to compose a mosaic design. Many artists use a "puzzle" technique, shaping and cutting each tile to fit together with other shaped tiles, just as the pieces of a puzzle or the parts of a stained glass window are made to fit together. The tiles at the top of this page were made in this manner.

Artists who use this technique must make design decisions as they divide their compositions into individual tile shapes. The *grout lines* (the spaces between the tiles which are later filled with grout) become very important; they provide the linear elements that define or outline objects in the composition. If you were to use this technique to depict a landscape and sky, for example, you might cut some of the tiles into the shapes of mountain peaks and divide the sky into cloud-shaped tiles that would fit around the mountains.

To design and make a mosaic this way, first make a line drawing of your full-sized design on a piece of large paper. Include and number each individual tile shape in your composition. Next, roll out a slab of clay as large as the composition—if the composition is small—or as large as one section if the composition itself is large. To impress the design lines into the clay, place the design paper on the slab and trace over the lines with a slightly blunted pencil. Remove the paper and cut out the tile shapes.

Rather than calculating shrinkage for grout line spaces, wait until the tile pieces that you cut from the large slab are leatherhard. The spaces left between the individual pieces once they've dried and are assembled will provide grout lines of roughly the correct size. If you need to make adjustments in order to make the grout lines wider, scrape the leatherhard tiles down so that the spaces between them are uniform.

As soon as you've cut the tile shapes, on the back of each one mark the number that corresponds to that tile's number in the drawing. This will make assembly of the finished tiles much easier. Sandwich the flat tiles between layers of wallboard so that they'll dry flat. Once the tiles are leatherhard, you may have to trim and reshape them.

The other, more traditional approach to making mosaics is to fill up each design element by arranging many shaped or broken pieces of tile. These small tile pieces can be cut from tiles that you have glazed and fired yourself or can be snipped from pieces of commercial tile. Look for damaged tiles at a tile store; these will come in a wide range of colors and will cost little or nothing. If you choose to glaze your own tiles and then nip pieces from them, you may want to glaze long strips of clay rather than squares or rectangles. The strips are easy to hold in one hand while you nip small pieces with the other.

Always wear safety glasses and thick gloves when snipping up tiles and use a good quality pair of *tile nippers*. Snipping with this sharp-jawed tool, which is similar to a pair of pliers, isn't easy, but with practice, you'll soon have buckets of categorized tile pieces with which to work. As you polish your nipping skills, keep in mind that traditional Islamic mosaic artisans cut the tiles with a chisel and hammer. In fact, skilled artisans specialize in cutting certain shapes, while the artist simply fills

Above and left: George F. Fishman
Faces of Flower Avenue. 1991
114" x 36" dia. (289.6 x 91.4 cm dia.)

Below: Nancy McCroskey
Aerial Rhythm. 1989
72" x 144" x 6" (182.9 x 365.8 x 15.2 cm)
Photograph by Bill Mills

John Bade
Mother and Child. 1986
48" x 48" x 1-1/4" (121.9 x 121.9 x 3.2 cm)
Photograph by Paul Kodama

Beth Katleman
Fallen Leaf Table (detail). 1992
30" x 42" x 26"
(76.2 x 106.7 x 66.0 cm)
Photograph by William Rivelli

in the design by selecting from among the shapes made for him.

Mosaic Assembly and Installation

Modern materials have provided the mosaic artist with some new tricks of the trade—here's one of them. First, purchase two grades of clear plastic adhesive film, one sticky and the other not very sticky (the "contact" paper sold in many hardware stores will do). Next, draw your design on a piece of paper and secure it to the table. Tack down a large piece of the less sticky film over your drawing, with the sticky side facing up. Arrange and fill in all the areas of your design by pressing the tile pieces onto the sticky paper; your design will show clearly through it. This film will keep your small mosaic pieces from sliding around if you bump the table as you work.

After you've completed the mosaic design, lay the stickier sheet of film face down on top of the tile pieces. Your tiles will now be sandwiched between the two layers, and you can transport them to the installation site without disturbing their positions.

To mount this sandwiched design, first turn the sandwich over so that the bottoms of the tiles face up. Then peel off the layer of less sticky film, which is now on top. Coat the back of the mosaic and the mounting surface with adhesive (see chapter 13). Lift the mosaic up by gripping the paper beneath it and position its

back against the mounting surface. As you do, the sticky film will continue to hold the mosaic pieces together. When the mosaic is in place, beat it smooth and flat against the mounting surface. After the adhesive has set, peel off the plastic film and apply grout.

If your design is large, you'll need to assemble and install the mosaic in manageable sections—perhaps 1' x 2' (30.5 cm x 61.0 cm) in size. Smaller mosaics of uniform thickness may be arranged on sheets of perforated paper, which are made for the tile industry in a variety of sizes—1' x 2' (30.5 cm x 61.0 cm), for example. Apply spray adhesive to one surface of the paper and arrange your mosaic pieces face up on the sticky surface. Coat the mounting surface with tile adhesive, and then press the mosaic, paper side down, directly against the mounting surface. The tile adhesive will spread through the perforations to the backs of the tile pieces.

For information on installation tools and adhesives, see chapter 13.

CHAPTER TWELVE

TILE DESIGN

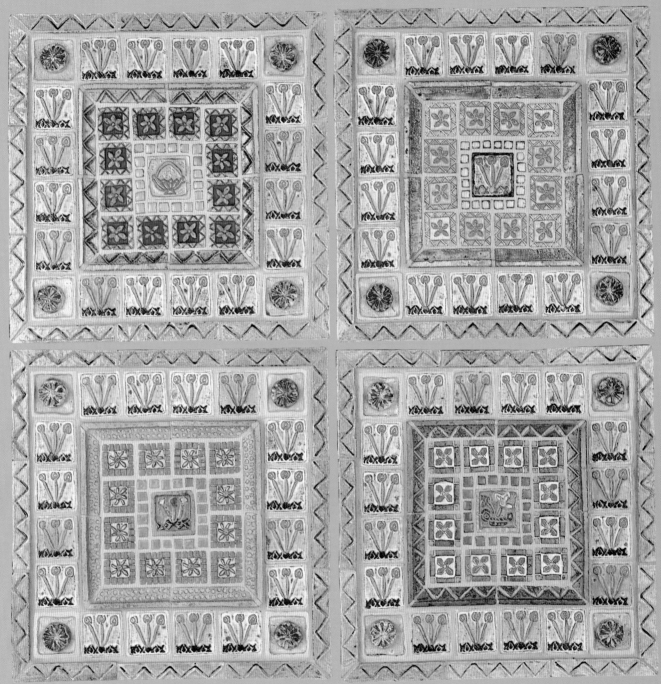

Mimi Strang
Window Box. 1990
37" x 37" x 2" (94.0 x 94.0 x 5.1 cm)

Above: Shel Neymark
Wildlife of the Rio Grande Window. 1991
60" x 42" x 9" (152.4 x 106.7 x 22.9 cm)
Photograph by Herb Lotz

Above left: Shel Neymark
Datura Fireplace. 1991
38" x 45" (96.5 x 114.3 cm)
Photograph by Herb Lotz

Below: Judith Williams
Flood Control Wall. 1989
72" x 800' (182.9 cm x 243.8 m)

Beth Starbuck
and Steven Goldner
Tile Table. 1988
25" x 40" x 20"
(63.5 x 101.6 x 50.8 cm)

Designing for Application

As you've probably realized by now, there are many ways to transform your ideas into finished tiles. Some of these have been explained to you, but now that you have a place from which to start, be inventive and develop some of your own. Your knowledge and craftsmanship will improve with experience.

Start with modest projects: a table top, tray, backsplash, or counter top. You'll learn most from your mistakes, and the many technical steps that make up the ceramic process leave plenty of room for those! Don't be discouraged. The rewards of success will outweigh the disappointments.

By identifying the design parameters before you begin a project, you'll improve your chances for success. Begin by asking yourself what function your tiles will serve. Will they be decorative or will they provide a waterproof, hygienic surface covering as well? Will they be installed indoors or out? Will they be in an environment that's always wet, such as a swimming pool, fountain, or shower? Will they be installed on the floor or wall?

The answers to these questions will help you to determine how hard and porous your clay needs to be and what sort of glaze to use on it. The ceramic industry has developed a standard code for rating the porosity and hardness of tiles in relation to their intended use. For a fee, the Tile Council of America (see page 142) will test a sample tile.

Following are some function-based guidelines to help you make design choices. Once you've decided on a flat or relief design, you may apply any one (or a combination) of the surface decoration techniques that you've learned—inlay, shellac resist, or sgraffiato, for example.

Table Tops, Counter Tops, and Backsplashes
Design type: Flat on counter tops; low-relief on backsplashes

Glazes and firing: Glazes necessary for hygiene, stain resistance, and ease of cleaning. Low-fire glazes adequate, but cone 2 bisque recommended. Stoneware clays and glazes are even better.

Fireplace Facades and Murals
Design type: Flat, low-relief, or high-relief

Glazes and firing: Glazes optional (probably unnecessary as a moisture barrier). Low-fire glazes adequate. Use cone 2 bisque for fireplaces because heavy objects such as wood and hearth tools may damage clay that's fired at lower temperatures. Stoneware clays and glazes are even better.

Walls in Dry Areas
Design type: Flat, low-relief, or high-relief as accents

Glazes and firing: Low-fire glazes adequate. Stoneware clays and glazes are even better.

Walls in Wet Areas (Showers, Pools, and Fountains)
Design type: Flat, low-relief tiles. High-relief tiles appropriate only when they won't prove hazardous upon bodily contact.

Glazes and firing: Glazed, low-fire clays adequate if vitreous. Stoneware clays and glazes are even better. Tile surfaces must be sealed against moisture with a glaze, and the clay body must be fired to vitrification. Sealers for the grout are available, but the less porous the clay body, the better.

Fired Earth Tiles
Provencal: Vert Ocean and Cinnamon with Cerise Border. On-going
Each 3-9/16" x 3-9/16" x 5/16"
(9.0 x 9.0 x .8 cm)

Floors

Design type: Flat tiles; flat, low-relief tiles.

Glazes and firing: Durability is important. The higher fired, stronger, and denser the clay, the better. Minimum of cone 2 temperature recommended. (Low-fire earthenware tiles, such as Mexican terra cotta, create a warm, rustic look but chip easily and are so porous that they must be sealed with waxes, oils, or chemicals. They also require regular maintenance.) Use matte or textured glazes; shiny ones may be too slippery, especially when wet. Encaustic tiles are a traditional choice.

Tile Designs

The first thing to consider when you're designing with tiles is that they may be around for a long time. Tiles are relatively expensive to make or to purchase, and once they're installed, they are difficult and expensive to remove. Create designs that are more than momentarily appealing, ones that will fit comfortably in their environment for years to come. Well-made and properly installed tiles can last for hundreds of years, so design for the long run, not for the short. If your tiles are too bizarre or trendy, you or your client will soon tire of them.

Tile sizes should match the scale of your environment. In general, the larger the room, the larger the tile. There are always exceptions to this rule, however; it's up to you to decide what tile size to use in a given space. Of course, you can create a pattern that has overall interest by working with various tile sizes and shapes.

More is not necessarily better. If you've created a boldly designed tile for a wall, pressing out hundreds of them to cover the entire wall area would probably be disastrous. The endless repetition of the individual tile design would diminish its visual impact.

A better way to highlight a special tile might be to feature it at preselected locations on the wall and surround it with flat background tiles. The unique tile, in this example, is referred to as an *accent tile*, and the surrounding background tiles are called *field tiles*. An accent tile that fits well in both size and color with less expensive, commercially available field tiles, is a very desirable product. And clients will probably be more willing to pay for expensive tiles when only a few are necessary to create a custom look for the total architectural environment.

Try to offer something unique in your designs and surface treatment. A great many beautiful and flawlessly made commercial tiles are already available. As an individual tile artist, you must therefore try to capitalize on your own talents—the creativity of your mind and the work of your hands. Add to that the love from your heart, and you will produce tiles that are objects of beauty for generations to come.

Computer Tile Design

If tile design becomes more than a part-time interest for you and you own a home computer, you may want to consider purchasing computer design software. Once you've installed this software, you'll have a graphics tool that lends itself extremely well to tile design (Photo 66).

66

Elizabeth Grajales
Snow Leopard (from the PS 92 Project,
Who Else Shares Our World). 1992
8" x 8" (20.3 x 20.3 cm)

Frank D'Amico
Untitled. 1993
11" x 12" (27.9 x 30.5 cm)
Photograph by Frank D'Amico

There are many advantages to using a computer for design purposes. The most important is that you'll save a great deal of time that would otherwise be spent drawing and redrawing designs by hand or running back and forth to a copy shop. A design program will allow you to create repeats, alternative design shapes, and design variations. It will also help you to resize design elements quickly, store them in a permanent "library," and combine or change them as you choose (Photo 67).

Your first step will be to select software for your home computer. Before you set off to do this, answer the following questions.

- *Is your computer a Macintosh, IBM, or IBM compatible?* You must know this because software is system specific. If you own an IBM or compatible, what size disks and drive do you use? IBM software is available on either 5.25" (13.3 cm) or 3.5" (8.9 cm) floppy disks. Macintosh software is available on 3.5" (8.9 cm) floppy disks and on CD-ROM.

Macintosh is a registered trademark of Apple Computer, Inc.

- *How much available RAM (or system memory) do you have in your computer?* Software differs in the amount of free system memory that it requires in order to operate. Unless you plan on adding more memory at the same time, don't buy software for which the RAM requirements exceed the memory now available on your computer.

- *If you have an internal hard drive, what is its capacity?* It's desirable to have an internal hard drive that can accommodate all of the software that you wish to install, with storage capacity for the files you create. An average hard drive is about forty megabytes in capacity, and the average drawing or painting software application will occupy two to six megabytes of available hard disk space.

- *How much time and money do you have to invest?* Some programs come with more features than others and may be time consuming to learn as well as expensive. Sometimes, a simpler, less expensive program will serve the novice's needs perfectly.

Types of Software: "Draw" vs. "Paint" programs

Draw programs create shapes by mathematically generating *vectors* (or points and curves). By moving and clicking a mouse, the user manipulates different tools to create shapes on-screen. These shapes can then be rotated, scaled, copied, and revised. Like paper cutouts, the shapes can be arranged in layers while you work on the design; moving or overlaying shapes will not alter the shapes themselves or what is behind them. The software can continually update the position of all items in the drawing.

Some software will also allow you to use scans of sketches as drawing templates. If, for example, you wanted to create a design based on a photo or drawing, you would first have a scan made up for you at a commercial service or make one yourself at a computer

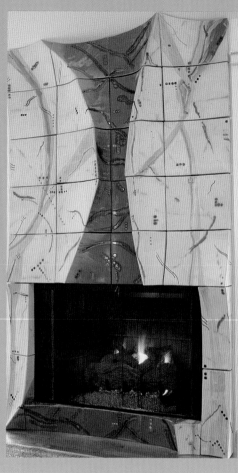

Diane Swift
Oak and Red-Tail Hawks.
1987
114" x 84" x 1/2" to 8"
(289.6 x 213.4 x
1.3 to 20.3 cm)
Photograph by John Woods

Beverlee Lehr
Moulton's Wall. 1993
90" x 60" x up to 7"
(228.6 x 152.4 x 17.8 cm)
Photograph by Carl Socolow

rental center—unless, of course, you own a scanner. Next, you would take the floppy disk containing the scan to your home computer. In the drawing program, you can open a *template*—a grayed version of your scan. This will function as a guide that you can use while you draw on-screen; the process is similar to drawing on a piece of tracing paper. (Note that the template will not print.) You'll even find programs that offer automatic template tracing.

Draw programs are well suited to tile design because designs with repeating elements can be made and revised easily and quickly and because prints from these programs (which you'll need in order to transfer your design), are smooth edged when printed from a laser printer, due to their mathematical description.

One disadvantage to draw programs, however, is that they take longer to master; the process of drawing with a mouse can be tricky. Another is that some draw programs don't work in the "preview" mode. If you wished to create a design with solid elements (outlined star shapes filled with color, for example), you would draw the outlines of those shapes and could only view them as outlines while actively drawing. You must stop drawing and preview the drawing to see its solid areas of color and different line weights. You can switch views as often as you like, but you can't draw and preview simultaneously unless you have two windows open at the same time.

Paint programs create shapes on a grid of *pixels* (or squares) that make up the page on your screen, much as colored tiles make up a mosaic. Programs that use the grids are also called *bitmap* programs. With a mouse, the user changes the colors of the squares in order to form shapes by drawing on-screen with a tool. You can start from scratch, or a pencil sketch can be scanned, opened with the paint software, and further developed with the program's painting and editing tools. Most paint programs also have copy, scale, and rotate commands of *selections* (groups of pixels). This can sometimes create problems, however, because to move the squares of a bitmap, you must literally pick up the pixels and displace them, leaving a hole behind. When you place the selection of pixels on top of another area, the pixels underneath are then erased. If you wish to enlarge a selection, a jagged appearance on the edges of the shape results, as if it were built of large squares instead of additional smaller squares. This is called *loss of resolution.* Resolution is also very important in printing from a paint program; low-resolution documents print poorly, with jagged lines and edges, while high-resolution files print better but tend to be large and to take a sizable amount of hard disk storage.

The advantage of paint programs is that their more direct method of operation is a little easier to master than that of draw programs. Their large disadvantage for tile design, however, is that once the designs are painted, they aren't as easy to revise or edit as are those created with draw programs.

Some software combines tools from drawing and painting programs into a single package, making it possible to experiment with elements of each.

Katy Cauker
Twist & Shout. 1988
54" x 30" x 1/2"
(137.2 x 76.2 x 1.3 cm)
Photograph by Kath Leen

Susan Beere (from design by Erik Voght)
Banana Leaf Mural. 1989
48" x 96" (121.9 x 243.8 cm)
Photograph by Hugh L. Wilkerson

Susan Beere
Egret's View. 1991
36" x 24" (91.4 x 61.0 cm)
Photograph by Hugh L. Wilkerson

To transfer a printed design to a plaster block for carving, use the nail-polish remover technique described on pages 52-53 but don't bother to get a photocopy. Your computer-printed design will work just as well.

The illustrations below demonstrate just a few of the ways in which design software can be used for tile designing. These designs were created with a high-end draw application.

Illustration 1. Tile design based on repetitions of a single design element.

Illustration 3. Tile design consisting of two repeated design elements. Note that only segments of these elements appear around the edges of the tile.

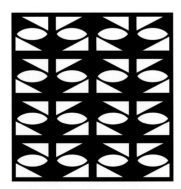

Illustration 2. Design variation based on design element shown in Illustration 1.

Illustration 4. The same tile pattern as shown in Illustration 3, printed in reverse.

CHAPTER THIRTEEN

INSTALLATION

Fired Earth Tiles
Terracotta Stones. On-going
Each 3-15/16" x 3-15/16" x 3/4" (10.0 x 10.0 x 2.0 cm)

Linda Dixon and Drew Krouse
Lion Fountain and *Mosaic Pool.* 1993
180" x 84" x 60"
(457.2 x 213.4 x 152.4 cm)
Photograph by LDDK Studios

Whether or Not to Try It

Now that you've made your tiles, what do you do with them? Designs that stand alone may be mounted just as pictures are. For instructions on making hangers, see chapter 14. Tiles, however, are really made to be installed on a permanent surface; only then do they fulfill their function as durable, decorative, hygienic surface coverings. When you see your tiles mounted and grouted as an intrinsic part of an architectural environment, you will really appreciate their worth.

Good installation can make mediocre tiles look great, and poor installation will make great tiles look mediocre, so don't skimp on installation costs. For a professional-looking job, hire a professional tile setter, one who has had experience with handmade tiles, which may be thicker, heavier, and more irregular than commercial tiles. Tile setting is an art in itself, one that has developed over generations; you're not likely to learn this highly specialized skill overnight.

If you're a skilled craftsperson who is competent with tools and experienced in construction techniques, you're certainly capable of learning how to install your own tiles, but you'll need to practice in order to become proficient. Working with an experienced tile setter will teach you many "tricks of the trade" that will make installation work proceed more easily and efficiently. Unless you are already versed in tile installation techniques, start with a relatively simple project such as the one covered in this chapter—a small table top.

Adhesives

Always use the correct type of adhesive material for the surface that you intend to cover.

- *Thinset adhesive* (or *mastic*) comes in 1-quart to 5-gallon (1.1 liter to 21.1 liter) containers and is used on drywall or on thoroughly cured concrete walls. It's not made for use on floors or plywood. Tiles installed with thinset must be completely dry and should be dry-cut with a tile cutter.

- *Multipurpose adhesive* can be used on drywall, cured concrete, or plywood, and is used for wall, floor, counter, and table-top installations. The tiles and the mounting surface must be dry and dust free. The premixed adhesive comes in amounts ranging from 1 quart to 5 gallons (1.1 liter to 21.1 liters) and is the best choice for a small project like a plywood table top.

- *Thinset cement*, which is mixed with water, is usually used on damp or wet concrete slabs, walls, or floors. The mounting surface, which is first wiped with a damp sponge to remove all dust, need not dry before the adhesive is installed. Because thinset cement will adhere to wet tiles, it is ideal for use on tiles cut with a wet saw. It comes in 50-pound (22.8 kg) bags and is mixed with water to a creamy consistency.

- *Thinset cement with a bonding agent* is just what it sounds like. The bonding agent is a

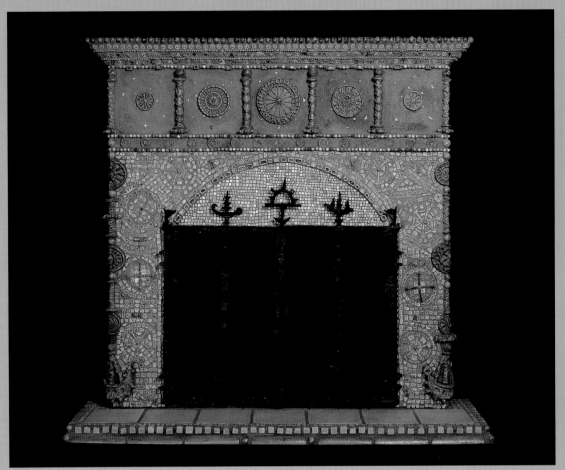

Gloria Kosco
Fireplace, #2. 1989
58" x 63" x 16"
(147.3 x 160.0 x 40.6 cm)
Photograph by John Hoenstine

milky-looking liquid that is mixed with thinset cement in a ratio of 2 gallons (8.5 liters) bonding agent to 50 pounds (22.8 kg) thinset. The bonding agent gives elasticity to the mixture, so that it will adhere to surfaces other than concrete—to plywood and sheetrock, for example. The mixture is very strong and can be used on either walls or floors.

- *Epoxy thinset* consists of three ingredients that must be mixed together: one-third Part A liquid epoxy, one-third Part B liquid epoxy, and one-third powdered filler. Epoxy thinset comes in quart (1.1 liter) and gallon (4.2 liter) packages and can be used on most dry surfaces. Because it's significantly more expensive than other adhesives, it's most often used for setting irregular tiles on metal. At one time, epoxy thinset was the strongest adhesive available, but thinsets with bonding agents are now just as strong.

- The term *mud set* refers to a traditional installation method in which tiles are set directly into *mud* (or wet cement). This is a craft with ancient origins, one that should only be attempted by a professional tile setter who is experienced in it. When executed correctly, mud setting is the most permanent installation method, as evidenced by ancient tile work that is still intact at historical sites such as Pompeii and Rome. Mud job

techniques are too involved for inclusion here, but detailed information on mud setting is available.

- *Grout* is a form of cement that is used to fill and seal the joints between installed tiles. Grouts come in various colors; white grout is traditionally used for walls, and a natural gray color, which won't show dirt, is often used on floors.

  Some grouts also contain sand. These are used for floor tiles, handmade tiles, and for any tile installation with wide grout lines. For high-gloss tiles and tile installations with narrow grout lines, use a grout without sand.

Tools

Every installation project has an element that's unique; your materials, tools, and techniques should be chosen accordingly.

- *Buttering trowels* are sturdy, spatula-like tools, which come in various sizes and shapes and which are usually made with pointed or squared-off blades. They are used to apply adhesive to the backs of tiles (a process known as *buttering*) or to transfer adhesive from a bucket to the mounting surface.

- *Toothed trowels*, used to spread the adhesive over the mounting surface, are usually rectangular and have toothed edges of various sizes and shapes (Photo 68). As the trowel is used, its teeth create

spaces between the raised beads of applied adhesive that are shaped by the tool's notches. Then, when the tile is pressed onto the adhesive bed, the adhesive spreads into these spaces. A 1/2" toothed trowel, therefore, will give a 1/4" adhesive bed once the tile is in place, and a 1/4" trowel will give a 1/8" bed. In general, the bigger and heavier the tiles, the larger the notches should be between the teeth of the trowel you select.

For handmade tiles, use a 1/4" to 1/2" (.6 cm to 1.3 cm) toothed trowel. If the back of the tile isn't completely flat, you may need to use a buttering tool to apply adhesive to the tile as well as to the mounting surface.

- *Rubber floats* are trowel-like tools with thick, soft rubber surfaces. They're used for spreading grout over and between the tiles.

- *Large sponges* and *buckets of water* should be kept on hand. You'll be cleaning surfaces and tools continually as you work.

- *Tile nips* are plier-like tools, the jaws of which have sharp, flat teeth. They're used to nip off small pieces from commercial tiles when you make a mosaic or to cut tiles to fit around obstructions such as pipes. Always wear safety glasses and heavy gloves when you use these tools.

  With thick handmade tiles, tile nips are less reliable and may crack the tile. A wet saw, a hand-held, diamond-tipped, rotary blade, or a jigsaw with a carbon blade may do a better job.

- *Tile cutters* have blades that snap straight cuts across thin, flat tiles. These tools may not work on handmade relief tiles, which are often too large, thick, or irregular for cutters to handle; it's best to use a wet saw instead.

- A *wet saw* is a tool for professionals; it's large and it can be expensive. In addition to cutting through tiles of almost any size or shape, a wet saw can easily cut beveled edges on the thickest of handmade tiles. When the tool is in use, its diamond-carbide blade is continuously lubricated with water.

- *Protective gloves* and a *mask* should always be worn when you work with chemical adhesives, cements, and grouts. If you work without gloves, your skin may dry out and crack, especially around the fingertips. Use a good hand lotion even if you do wear gloves. An approved dust and mist mask is also a must whenever you work with cement; the cement-mixing process creates clouds of dust.

- *Clean-up materials* should be kept handy. Make sure that you have plenty of sponges, buckets of

Opposite page, left: Frank Giorgini
Ribbed System. 1993
Each 6" x 6" (15.2 x 15.2 cm)

Photograph by Bobby Hansson

Opposite page, right:
Susan E. Kowalczyk
Untitled; earthenware floor detail.
1985
120" x 120" (304.8 x 304.8 cm)

Photograph by David H. Ramsey

Above: Shel Neymark
Deco Sideboard Table and Lamp.
1989
Table: 30" x 14" x 60"
(76.2 x 35.6 x 152.4 cm)
Lamp: 28" h. (71.1 cm)

Photograph by Mark Kane

Right: Peter King and Marni Jaime
Mizneresque. 1992
70" x 74" (177.8 x 188.0 cm)

Photograph by Gary Langhammer

Above: Mathers Rowley
Caribbean Coral Reef Scene (detail). 1992
Overall: 84" x 276" (213.4 x 701.0 cm)

Left: Peter Sohngen
Building Blocks (detail). 1991
29" x 37" (73.7 x 94.0 cm)

Opposite page: Elyse Saperstein
Legends (detail). 1990
32" x 120" x 2" (81.3 x 304.8 x 5.1 cm)
Photograph by John Carlano

water, and towels. Clean all your tools with water as soon as you're finished with them, or the installation materials will harden, and removal will be nearly impossible. Most of the materials are water soluble and will be easy to remove if you act quickly.

Installation on a Table Top

The instructions that follow can be applied to installing handmade tiles on almost any horizontal surface.

Before you cut your plywood table top to size, it's important to create a layout and to estimate the width of the grout lines. Traditionally, tiles are set with a grout joint between them that is the thickness of a trowel blade—1/16" (.16 cm). Most handmade tiles, however, are irregular in size, so the grout lines must be wider.

To determine the width of these joints, first arrange at least one square foot (929.0 sq. cm) of tiles next to each other, using a framing square to square them off. If this square shape is 1/8" (.3 cm) off square, you'll need a 1/4"-wide (.6 cm) grout joint. If the shape is 1/4" (.6 cm) off square, you'll need a 1/2" (1.3 cm) grout joint. This method will ensure that the irregular edges of the tiles will fall within straight-lined grout joints.

Next, determine the layout of your tiles, allowing for the width of the grout lines between them, by arranging them on a piece of 3/4"-thick plywood. (For very complex designs made up of irregularly shaped tiles, it would be wise to lay out the entire design before starting.) As you do this, consider the edges of the table top. One way to create an edge for your table is to attach strips of 3/4"-thick (1.9 cm) plywood around the bottom edges of the table top; these will provide a base against which you can glue and nail strips of corner molding (see Illustration 1). To trim your table top's edges with narrow tiles, place the outermost tiles on the plywood's upper surface so that they overlap the plywood's outer edges by the width of the narrow

edges of the tiles that will adhere vertically to the table's edge (see Illustration 2). Arranging the tiles in this manner will strengthen the edges.

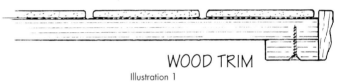

WOOD TRIM
Illustration 1

Illustration 2 **TILE TRIM**

Once your layout is complete and allows for all tiles and grout lines, cut the 3/4"-thick (1.9 cm) plywood to the desired size of the table top. Use carpenter's glue and screws to attach four strips of 3/4"-thick (1.9 cm) plywood, 2" to 3" (5.1 cm to 7.6 cm) in width to the bottom surface, as shown in Illustration 3.

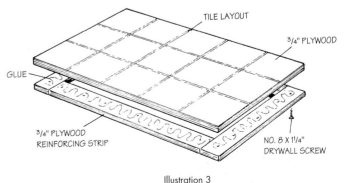

TILE LAYOUT

3/4" PLYWOOD

GLUE

3/4" PLYWOOD REINFORCING STRIP

NO. 8 X 1¼" DRYWALL SCREW

Illustration 3

Before installing your tiles, make sure that the back of each one and the table top itself are free of dust and completely dry.

Then apply a 1/8"- to 1/4"-thick (.3 cm to .6 cm)—depending on the thickness of the tile—layer of multi-purpose ceramic adhesive to the surface of the table (and to its edges if you'll be placing tiles on them). Press the tiles down onto the plywood. Note in Photos 69 and 70 that rather than spreading adhesive over

the entire table top and risk having it dry out as he works, the installer is setting the edge sections first. If your tiles are warped, you'll need to butter (apply

adhesive to) the back of each tile as well as to the mounting surface.

If your tiles differ in thickness, install the thickest tiles first and then build the adhesive up behind the thin-

Mix your grout with water (or, for greater strength, a grout-bonding agent) in a clean bucket until the mixture is the consistency of whipped cream. Then pour the

ner tiles so that their top surfaces are level with those of the thicker tiles. If your tiles are all the same thickness, you need only apply adhesive to the plywood, using a toothed trowel held at a 45° angle and spreading only as much as can be covered with tiles within twenty minutes (Photos 72 and 73). Press the tiles down into the adhesive (Photo 74) until the table top is covered.

If you accidentally get adhesive on a tile's surface, just use a sponge dampened with hot water to wipe it off lightly (Photo 75). Be careful not to get any water into the grout joints as you do this. After all the tiles are installed, allow twenty-four hours for the adhesive to dry.

Allow the grout to set for approximately fifteen minutes and then wash the surface of the table with a damp sponge and water, smoothing out the grout joints as you do (Photo 79). Continue to clean the table, removing the grout from your sponge by rinsing it in a bucket of water (Photo 80). When the surface is clean, allow twenty-four hours for the grout to dry. Then buff the table top with a dry rag to remove the film of grout on it (Photo 81).

During this entire process, remember to clean your tools while the adhesive or grout on them is still damp.

required amount onto the table top (Photo 76). With a rubber float or a rubber squeegee held at a 45° angle, spread the grout over the tiles, pressing it into the joints (Photos 77 and 78). To remove excess grout from the tiles' upper surfaces, scrape across the tiles with a rubber float or squeegee, moving the tool at a diagonal to the grout joints.

CHAPTER FOURTEEN

MAKING YOUR OWN
TOOLS AND EQUIPMENT

Carrie Anne Parks
Peaches. 1991
29" x 23-1/2" x 6"
(73.7 x 59.7 x 15.2 cm)

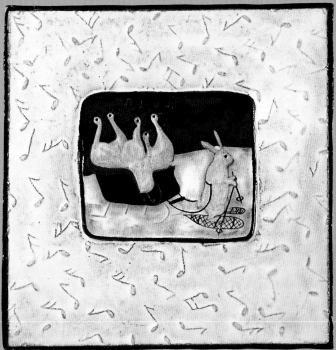

Ellie Hudovernik
Snowshoe Rabbit with Carolling Geese. 1st Annual Christmas Tile. 1993
4-3/4" x 4-3/4" (12.1 x 12.1 cm)
Photograph by Robert Hudovernik

Frank Giorgini
Afro Tile. 1986
14" x 14" (35.6 x 35.6 cm)
Photograph by Bobby Hansson

Due to the large number of dimensions given in this chapter, metric conversions are not provided. For readers who are more comfortable with the metric system, conversion charts are provided on page 143.

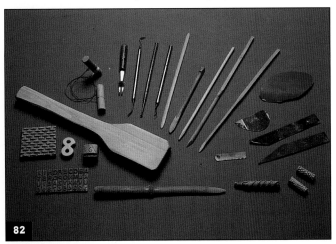

Materials

Making things that will help you with your tile work is easy, fun, and a great way to recycle those odds and ends around the house that might otherwise end up at your local landfill. Though you'll need to purchase materials to make some of the tools described in this chapter, many of the others can be made from common household items. A few wire coat hangers, tin cans, and plastic jugs will yield more than you might think. With the help of the instructions that follow, you can transform them all into handy workshop items.

Cut-Off Wire

To make a cut-off wire (shown in the upper left-hand corner of Photo 82), just thread a 20" length of wire or monofilament fishing line through holes drilled in two objects that will serve as grips—short lengths of dowel will work well. Guitar strings make good substitutes for fishing line or wire.

Templates

Templates—cut to the size and shape of your tiles—can be cut from thin plywood, Masonite, or cardboard. To use a template, just place it on your clay slab and scribe or cut around it with your pin tool. Don't forget to calculate shrinkage before cutting your templates to size.

Storage Containers

Recycled glass and plastic containers with lids make fine storage containers for mixed stains, glazes, and powders. The top portions of some plastic bottles make excellent funnels, too; just cut them off and invert them. Use the lower sections of the bottles as water containers.

Sculpting, Incising, and Scraping Tools

Photo 82 shows a number of these easy-to-make tools.

- Chopsticks make excellent sculpting tools. The bamboo from which they're made is durable, and clay won't stick to it either. Chopsticks are usually free for the asking. Whittle the ends into a variety of useful shapes (Illustration 1) and finish them off with fine sandpaper. If you have access to an electric grinder or sander, you can turn out several in no time at all. To use these tools, push and shape the clay with their ends.

- *Metal strapping*—the strong, steel banding material that is used to wrap heavy materials such as lumber and large crates—makes wonderful

Right: Cairo Cocalis
Birds' Feet. 1992
Each 4" x 4" (10.2 x 10.2 cm)
Photograph by Elizabeth Vanderkooy

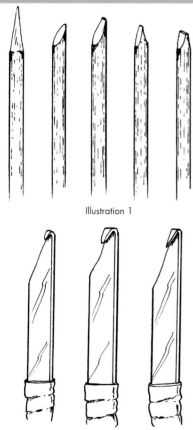

Illustration 1

Illustration 2

incising tools. Many commercial shippers have switched to strong plastic straps, but you can still locate steel strapping if you ask around.

Wear thick gloves and goggles when you fabricate these metal tools; flat metal is very sharp. Cut several 6" to 8" lengths of strapping. Using a file or grinder, sharpen one end of each length to knife-

blade sharpness. Then, with a pair of needle-nose pliers, carefully bend the sharpened ends into different shapes (Illustration 2). Do this slowly, as the metal is brittle and may snap. Wrap some tape around the other end, and you'll have a very efficient tool for carving fine grooved lines into your leatherhard tiles. This tool is perfect for use in the incising and inlay techniques.

• Scraping tools can be made from all sorts of scrap metal, including tin cans (Illustration 3). With metal shears, cut an oval rib shape from the side of a can; wear gloves while you do this. Flatten out the shape with a hammer and then file, sand, or grind the edges smooth.

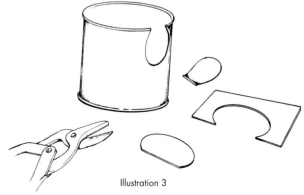

Illustration 3

• Scrapers can also be cut from plastic containers. A heavy pair of scissors will cut through most thinner, pliable plastics, but you may need a saw to cut plastic that's thicker and more rigid. Avoid using sharp knives for this job; it's all too easy to slip and cut yourself with one. Sand the edges of these cut shapes as well.

• To make a special tool for scraping beads of glaze from the edges of a tile (Illustration 4), use either a piece of metal strapping or a piece of tin can. Just cut a 90° notch in the strapping or tin. When you run this tool along the bottom edge of the tile, the notch will remove the glaze evenly.

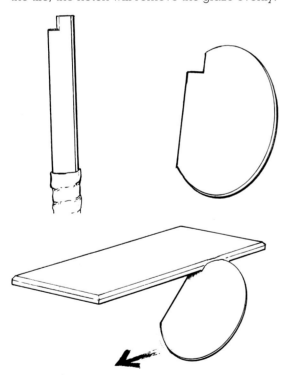

Illustration 4

• Hacksaw blades can be shaped into excellent scraping and sculpting tools. These blades, which are used to cut metal, are usually about 12" long and 1/2" wide and have very fine teeth. First, be sure that you're wearing some form of eye protection and gloves. Then take a pair of pliers and snap off a 2" length of blade; you shouldn't have any trouble breaking this brittle metal. Use your new tool to scrape and smooth

convex surfaces. To shape contours on moist or leatherhard clay, first scrape at a 45° angle to the curve and then scrape at the opposite 45° angle, so that the two scraping angles are perpendicular to each other. Alternating directions in this manner will produce a beautiful contoured surface.

This tool is also very useful for scraping smooth, recessed flat surfaces on your tiles. The rough surfaces left by its teeth can be smoothed.

• Dental tools are very helpful when you're completing detail work. Ask your dentist if he or she has any tools that have one broken end; these rejects, no longer useful to the dentist, may be yours for the asking.

• If you have access to a grinder, even the tips of 3"-long nails can be easily ground into useful shapes.

Tile Dipper

With one coat hanger and a pair of pliers or metal snips, you can fabricate a tool that's perfect for dipping your tile into glaze. To make this long, V-shaped dipping tool, first cut and remove the hook from a heavy-gauge wire hanger. Straighten out both arms of the V and cut them to equal lengths. Then bend up about 1/2" of wire at the end of each arm to create a 90° (or greater) angle.

For larger tiles, use a whole hanger to make a longer dipper. If the tile is too big and heavy to be held in the tool just described, use a length of 1 x 2 or a strip of 1/2"-thick plywood with a couple of screws, nails, or dowels at the bottom to support the bottom edge of the tile.

Hanging Devices for Tiles

An excellent device for hanging and displaying individual tiles can be made from coat-hanger wire; thicker-gauged wire will work best for heavier tiles. Cut the hooks off three wire hangers and straighten each remaining length. Then cut the straightened lengths to size and bend them as shown in Illustration 5, in propor-

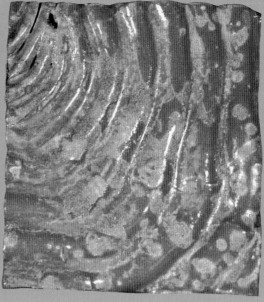

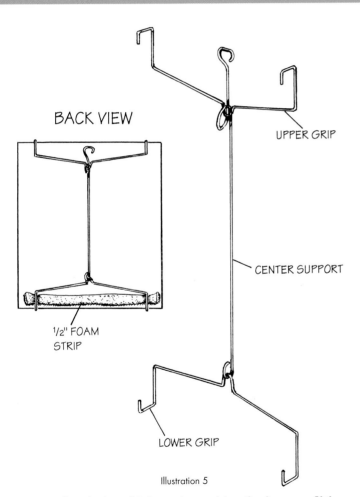

BACK VIEW

UPPER GRIP

CENTER SUPPORT

1/2" FOAM STRIP

LOWER GRIP

Illustration 5

it on a piece of plywood, as shown below. Cut a piece of 1/2"-thick plywood, about 1/2" to 1-1/2" smaller than your tile. Using a hole saw in an electric drill, cut a 1/2" to 2" diameter hole in the upper middle area of the wood. Drill two holes into the bottom edge of the plywood, about 1" in from each side. Place two "L" hooks in these holes to support the bottom edge of the tile. To gauge the hook depth correctly, carefully center the plywood on the back of your tile. Then turn the "L" hooks into their holes until they touch the tile's bottom edge. For a more finished appearance, spray paint the edges of the wood.

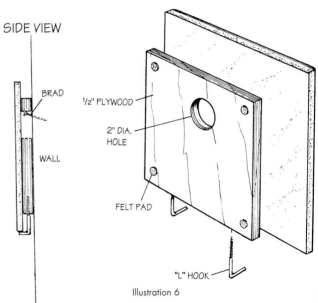

SIDE VIEW

BRAD

1/2" PLYWOOD

2" DIA. HOLE

WALL

FELT PAD

"L" HOOK

Illustration 6

tion to the tile for which you're making the hanger. If the hanger fits your tile too loosely, bend its top and bottom arms back on themselves to add some tension.

Wedging a strip of 1/2" foam between the lower back of the tile and the wire support will ensure that the tile hangs parallel to the wall and doesn't tilt to the left or right. To protect the front surface of your tile, slip small lengths of clear plastic tubing (available at hardware or pet stores) over the hooked ends of the wire.

Another way to display an individual tile is to mount

Affix the tile to the plywood with multipurpose adhesive, silicone glue, or any good tile adhesive, pushing the tile down so that its bottom edge rests on the hooks. These hooks will counter the force of gravity that will always pull on your tile. When the glue is dry, hang your tile by placing the hole over a nail. A few stick-on felt pads placed on the back of the wood will protect the wall. Because the tips of the two bottom hooks will be barely visible, the tile will appear to float on the wall.

Opposite page, left: Dianna Rose
Lightning Woman. 1990
12" x 12" (30.5 x 30.5 cm)
Photograph by Linda Pearson

Opposite page, right: Dianna Rose
Woman of Many Lands, Woman of Many Robes. 1992
12" x 12" (30.5 x 30.5 cm)
Photograph by James Marks

Left: Frank Giorgini
Chameleons in the Night. 1984
Mounted mural: 28" x 42" (71.1 x 106.7 cm)
Photograph by John Lawrence

Mural Hanger

The long beveled strips on the wall and mural-hanging device shown in Illustration 7 serve to distribute the mural's weight evenly against the mounting surface.

To construct this mounting board, first select a good grade of 3/4"-thick plywood that is finished on one side. Lay your mural out on the finished side, allowing for grout spaces if applicable, and trace around its perimeter. Square off the sides and then cut the plywood to size.

Next, reinforce the panel by using countersunk wood screws of an appropriate length to attach four 3/4" x 3" strips of plywood to the rear of the plywood mounting board. Cut two equal lengths from the same strip material and cut a 45° bevel along one long edge of each. Attach one strip to the back of the plywood, with its beveled edge facing down, and the other to the mounting surface, with its beveled edge facing up. Be

sure that the strip on the mounting surface is attached to the studs in the wall. To mount your completed mural, just rest one beveled strip along the beveled edge of the other, and gravity will hold the mural hanger in place.

To make a more attractive mural hanger, first refer to the photograph above, entitled *Chameleons in the Night.* Note that the tiles, which are set back about 1/2" from the aluminum frame around them, rest on plywood that has been painted black. The plywood back of this hanging device was cut 1" wider and 1" longer than the temporarily assembled mural tiles. A frame was then welded from 1/4"-thick, 2" aluminum angle stock; it was just large enough to enable me to drop the plywood back right into its interior. The frame was attached to the back of the plywood with screws.

A wooden reinforcement frame was attached to the back. This was made with strips of wood that would allow the aluminum frame to set at the desired height in relation to the thickness of the mounted tiles. A thicker beveled strip was attached to its back, to allow for the aluminum frame. I added a second strip to keep the bottom of the mural from tilting back against the wall.

Tools for Cutting Shapes from Slabs

If you're handy and have access to certain tools, it's not terribly difficult to make "cookie cutter" devices (Photo 83) with which to cut tile shapes from a clay slab. Don't forget to take tile shrinkage into account as you design the tools' final shapes and dimensions. And put on a pair of thick gloves; working with metal can be dangerous.

First, cut a piece of 3/4"-thick scrap wood to the shape that you'd like your tile to be. Use screws to attach a thin metal strip (the galvanized metal from which heating ducts are made works well) around the outer edges of the wooden shape and flush with its top surface. Make sure that the strip is wide enough to cut through the clay slab and that all corners are bent

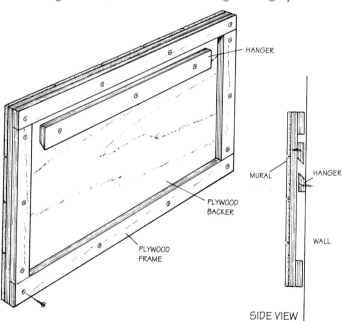

HANGER

MURAL   HANGER

PLYWOOD
BACKER

PLYWOOD
FRAME

WALL

SIDE VIEW

Illustration 7

83

cleanly. Because your slab is likely to be 3/8" to 1/2" thick, the strip should be about 2" wide.

To make a plunger mechanism that will release your cut tiles from the cutter, first drill a couple of 1/2" holes through the wood shape. Then insert two 3"-long dowels, each 1/2" thick, through the holes. Cut a Masonite or thin plywood template that is just a bit smaller than the wood shape and position it on the bottom of the shape so that it's surrounded by the metal edging material; it should be loose enough to have some play. Attach the Masonite to the dowels with countersunk screws. To make a handle for the plunger, fasten a strip of wood to the two dowels. Many variations of this design are possible.

Plaster-Block Mold Forms

Following are directions for making two types of mold forms. The first is used to make a plaster mold from an original relief tile. The second is a form with which you can produce several plaster blocks at a time for carving and pressing out relief tiles. (See chapters 5 and 6 for descriptions of these pressing techniques.)

Open-Face Mold Forms

To make a mold form for a handmade relief tile, first refer to Photo 22 on page 44. In the upper left-hand corner of this photograph is an adjustable mold form called a cottle. It is made from 3/4" x 8" x 20" pieces of counter-top material, the smooth Formica sides of which face inward. (Cottles can vary in size and in the materials from which they're made.) To one end of each cottle is fastened a 3/4" x 1-1/2" x 8" piece of wood; scraps of the counter-top board can also be used to make these blocks. Use glue and No. 6 x 1-1/4" countersunk wood screws to secure these blocks, making sure to fasten them to the outside surfaces of the cottle pieces.

When you're ready to make a plaster mold, position two of the cottle boards on edge and fasten them with a C-clamp. Take care not to let go of the boards as you do this, or they'll fall right on top of your model. Then fasten the remaining boards with three more C-clamps, adjusting the boards so that they form an enclosed area that is large enough to allow for a 1-1/2" to 2" space between the inner surface of each wall and the outer edge of the relief tile. Check the cottle for square and make sure that the tile model is equidistant from all four inner surfaces of the form. Then seal the bottom edges and corners of the form, as described in chapter 5.

Mold forms may also be made by cutting beveled lengths of 2 x 4 to specific lengths for specific tile projects and holding them together with a web or band clamp. The forms shown on the right-hand side of Photo 22 on page 44 consist of four 13"-long (O.D.) lengths of 2 x 4 that have been cut to allow for a 1-3/4" space between the inner walls of the form and the edges of the tile model. Each end of each piece is beveled at 45°. Place the lengths on edge and strap them together with a web (or band) clamp. Note that this form is not adjustable.

To calculate the dimensions of these forms, start with the dimensions of your tile model—4-1/2" x 4-1/2", for

example. Add between 3" and 4" to each dimension—the combined distance between the edges of the tile model and two opposing sides of the form. This figure (8", for example) will give you the inner dimensions of the form. Cut a 45° end on your 2 x 4, measure and mark the calculated length on its short face, flip the 2 x 4 over, and cut another 45° angle at the mark you made to give you a cottle wall of the correct length for your tile model. Repeat these steps to make the other three walls.

Mold Forms for Making Multiple Plaster Blocks

In order to carve plaster molds for relief tiles (see chapter 6), you'll need solid plaster blocks. Following are instructions for a time-saving form with which you can make several of these blocks at one time. The form consists of two notched lengths of Formica-coated wood, plastic, or Plexiglass that are held together with threaded rods and spacer strips that form multiple sections once they're placed between the notched lengths (Illustration 8). The form can also be made with plywood that has been well coated with polyurethane or clear wood sealer.

Shown in the foreground of Photo 22 on page 44 is a form that I made from 1/4"-thick scrap Plexiglass. When cutting Plexiglass, protect yourself against airborne shards by wearing protective clothing, gloves, and goggles. Formica is a safer alternative, and the plaster will

release from it very well because Formica is so smooth. When kitchen counter tops are made, the kitchen sink cutouts are often discarded. Try to find a couple of these scraps at a cabinet shop.

Before constructing this form, you will need to calculate shrinkage for the tiles that you'll be making with your plaster blocks; once you've made this calculation, you can determine the correct size of each square in the form.

The cross pieces can be made from any one of several materials. To make them from Formica, glue the backs of two Formica strips together so that their smooth sides are facing out. Masonite or lattice can also be used; just be sure to coat wood surfaces with polyurethane. Sheets of 1/8"-thick plastic are also available at hardware stores. These make excellent cross pieces because their width is the same as the width of most crosscut saw blades; making a notch for one in the side piece is as easy as making a single pass with the blade. The sheets are cut with a craft-knife blade designed for cutting plastic.

Cut two side pieces, each about 2' long and 2" wide. Then cut notched grooves, about 3/16" deep and as wide as the cross pieces that will be fit into them, making sure to cut these on the smooth face of each side piece. The dimensions between the notches on each side piece should equal the width of your plaster

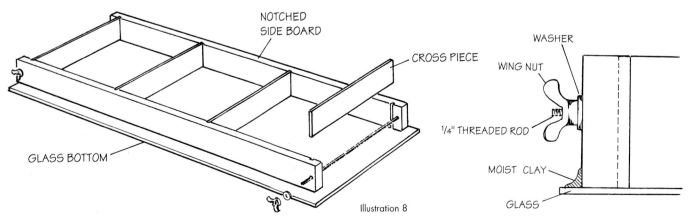

NOTCHED SIDE BOARD

CROSS PIECE

GLASS BOTTOM

WASHER

WING NUT

1/4" THREADED ROD

MOIST CLAY

GLASS

Illustration 8

Opposite page, left: Elizabeth Grajales
Pangolin (from the PS 92 Project,
Who Else Shares Our World). 1992
8" x 8" (20.3 x 20.3 cm)

Opposite page, right: Fired Earth Tiles
Harvest Borders & Harvest Bee Decor. Ongoing
4-5/16" x 2-1/2" x 3/8" and 4-5/16" x 4-5/16" x 3/8"
(11.0 x 6.0 x .9 cm and 11.0 x 11.0 x .9 cm)

Laird Plumleigh
Octopus. 1990
22-1/2" x 22-1/2" x 4" (57.2 x 57.2 x 10.2 cm)
Photograph by Phillip Ritterman

block. When you cut the cross pieces to size, remember to add the depth of the notches on each side to their length, or two sides of your plaster block will be shorter than you'd like.

Then center and drill 1/4" holes through each side piece, 3/4" from each end. Place the pieces on edge, lining them up so that the notched surfaces face each other.

Cut two lengths of 1/4" threaded rod to fit through the holes drilled in the side pieces; these should be long enough to accommodate a washer and wing nut on each end. Insert the rods into the drilled holes, slip the cross strips into the notches, and gently tighten the wing nuts until the strips are secure. Check to see that the corners of the form are all square. Then place the assembled form on a thick sheet of glass and use moist clay to seal the outside edges between the form and the glass as well as the outside corners.

Tile-Waxing Stand

This handy device (Illustration 9) will help you to wax the lower edges of your tiles in preparation for dipping the tiles into the glaze. You'll place the tile (face up) on the foam-padded platform and then use one hand to apply the wax with a foam brush as you use the other to rotate the stand on a turntable. Next, you'll lift the tile off the stand, hold it upside-down in one hand, and use the foam brush to wax the entire back.

When you're waxing many tiles, using the stand to support the tile during the first stage of the waxing process helps to keep your supporting arm from getting tired. Keeping the tile flat and face up keeps the wax from running across the surface that you want to glaze; gravity carries the wax down toward the bottom of the tile instead.

To build this simple stand, first rip an approximately 24"-long piece of 1-3/4" x 3-1/2" pine into two 1-3/4"-wide lengths. One of these pieces will serve as the post; cut it to a length that will be comfortable for you once the completed stand is sitting on the turntable—perhaps 18". From the other piece, cut a 10" length to

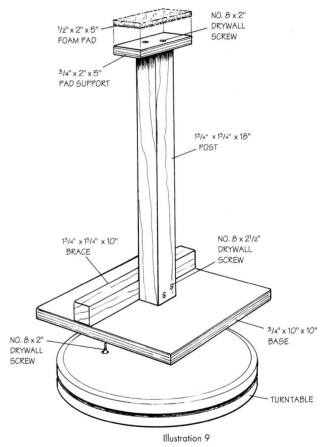

1/2" x 2" x 5"
FOAM PAD

NO. 8 x 2"
DRYWALL
SCREW

3/4" x 2" x 5"
PAD SUPPORT

1 3/4" x 1 3/4" x 18"
POST

1 3/4" x 1 3/4" x 10"
BRACE

NO. 8 x 2 1/2"
DRYWALL
SCREW

NO. 8 x 2"
DRYWALL
SCREW

3/4" x 10" x 10"
BASE

TURNTABLE

Illustration 9

serve as the brace. Then, to make the base, cut a 10" x 10" x 3/4" piece of plywood or pine. The foam support is also cut from 3/4"-thick wood; its width and length should be 1" smaller than the tiles on which you're working. For 3" x 6" tiles, for example, cut a 2" x 5" foam support. Finally, cut a piece of 1/2"-thick foam to the size of the foam support.

To assemble the waxing stand, first position the brace on the base so that one of its sides will be flush against the base of the center post once it's attached. Fasten it in place with two No. 8 x 2" drywall screws, inserted from the bottom of the base. Then center the

Opposite page, left:
Diana and Tom Watson
Brentwood Plaza
Stair Risers. 1993
Each 4-1/2" x 4-1/2"
(11.4 x 11.4 cm)
Photograph by Diana Watson

Hanna Lore Hombordy
Round Shell Tile. 1989
12" diameter (30.5 cm diameter)
Photograph by Hanna Lore Hombordy

Andrea Rudner
Star Mosaic. 1993
Image: 7" x 9" (17.8 x 22.9 cm)

post in the middle of the base with one face against the brace. Fasten the post to the brace with No. 8 x 2-1/2" drywall screws, as shown in the illustration. Also insert one screw through the bottom of the base and into the center post. To attach the foam support to the top of the post, center it on the post and then insert two No. 8 x 2" drywall screws through its face. Glue the foam to the support with rubber cement.

Slab Cutter

Used to cut small, tile-sized slabs of clay that are uniform in thickness, this tool is my own invention and makes the process of cutting multiple slabs quite easy. Its operating principle, depicted in Photo 84, is simple. The tool is placed on a block of clay and the cut-off wire is pulled across the metal edges of the tool to slice off slabs of a thickness determined by the distance between the edge of the angle irons and the bottom surface of the Masonite pad attached to the underside of the base. For specific instructions on how to use the slab cutter, see page 48.

On this particular model, constructed from scrap materials, I used 8"-long, 90° angle irons to create the metal edges across which the wire is pulled. As an alternative to the angle irons, I could have attached 1/4"-thick lattice strips or thin metal strips to the two edges of the 6" x 8" base. By doing this, I could easily change the thickness of my slabs whenever I wanted to, just by exchanging those strips for others of a different width. For my purposes, however—the production of six hundred identical tiles—the angle irons worked well.

To make sure that each slab was cut to a particular thickness, I attached a piece of Masonite (slightly longer and wider than the slabs I wanted to cut) to the underside of the base. (The pad is visible in Illustration 10 but not in Photo 84.) The 7/8" width of an angle iron's arm minus the 1/8" thickness of the pad equalled the 3/4" thickness of my desired slab.

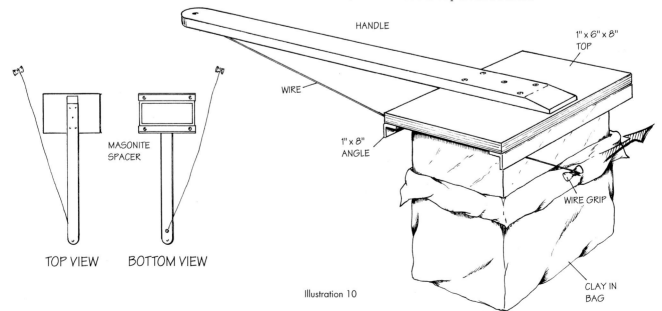

HANDLE

WIRE

1" x 6" x 8"
TOP

1" x 8"
ANGLE

WIRE GRIP

CLAY IN
BAG

MASONITE
SPACER

TOP VIEW   BOTTOM VIEW

Illustration 10

Dale Wiley
Scarab. 1987
5" x 5-3/4" (12.7 x 14.6 cm)
Photograph by Peter von Wilken Zook

84

site end of the handle, drill a 1/4" hole through the handle's face. Measure and mark a point centered 3-1/2" from the same end and insert a small screw eye at that point, with the eye in the handle's bottom surface.

Fasten the handle to the base with five countersunk No. 6 x 1-1/4" wood screws. Then fasten one end of the wire to the screw eye. Monofilament line makes a good substitute; though it will wear out more quickly, it won't fray as braided wire will. Cut the wire's other end so that about 12" of wire extends beyond the base. To make a grip for the wire, wrap this loose end around a short length of dowel. Loop some wire or string through the hole in the handle's end so that you can hang the slab cutter up when it's not in use.

Giorgini Studio Tile Press

The tile press featured in Photos 85 and 86 is my original design. It's used to press out tiles from either carved-block or open-face molds. For instructions on how to use it, refer to chapter 6.

The design is based on that of traditional manual presses used by tile manufacturers around the turn of

Apart from the dimensions that determine the thickness of the slabs to be cut, the dimensions of the other parts of this tool may vary quite a bit. The handle does need to be long enough to allow the wire to cut across the entire block of clay. I used a 24" long 1 x 3 furring strip. The base is 6" x 8", but these dimensions may be smaller or larger depending upon the desired size of the slabs.

If you use lattice strips rather than angle irons, you can avoid splitting the lattice as you attach it to the edges of the base by predrilling holes in it before inserting the 3/4" wood screws. If you do use angle irons, attach them to the base with 1/2"-long screws.

Though the dimensions of your slab cutter's parts may vary, the assembly procedure is fairly straightforward. Attach the angle irons, lattice strips, or metal strips to the base first. If you use the angle irons, center and glue the Masonite pad to the underside of the base, making sure that its smooth surface faces outward.

One end of the handle may be beveled at 45°, as shown in Photo 84, but this step isn't necessary. Mark locations for the five screws that will fasten the handle to the base. Then, centered about 1-1/2" from the oppo-

85

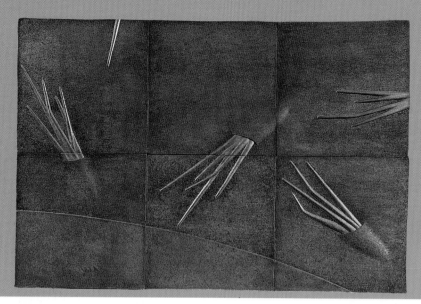

Opposite page: Jerry Wellman
Portraits (detail). 1993
Each 4-1/4" x 4-1/4"
(10.8 x 10.8 cm)

Frank Giorgini
Sea Life. 1985
Mounted mural: 28" x 42" (71.1 x 106.7 cm)
Photograph by John Lawrence

the century. Pressure applied by means of a simple lever-and-plunger mechanism serves to press moist clay into (or onto) a plaster mold. To see a similar press in operation, visit the Moravian Tile Works in Doylestown, Pennsylvania. The model there is larger and heavier than this one and requires some welding to construct.

Expensive hydraulic studio presses with air-pressure release molds are available, as are plans for making one yourself, but they're more complex to build than mine, and each air-release mold that you make for one of these presses takes a considerable investment. For greater production capability, however, they are useful.

This design can be made from standard lumber and plywood and from pipe fittings that are available from any hardware or plumbing supply store. Only simple hand tools and readily available hardware are required. The lightweight press, which will outperform most commercially available hand presses, is also

compact; it takes up only two feet of counter space. And it's durable, too. In fact, the original model has been in service at Parsons School of Design for eight years and has not required any maintenance or repair.

Suggested Tools
Circular saw
Jigsaw or saber saw
3/8" Variable-speed drill
7/64" Drill bit
1-1/4" Spade bit
Countersink bit
No. 2 Phillips screwdriver
No. 2 Phillips power-drive bit
3/16" Straight-bladed screwdriver
Hammer
Round wood rasp
Tape measure
24" Straightedge
Pipe wrenches
Sandpaper
Safety goggles

Required Lumber
1	3/4" x 4' x 4'	C-D Plywood or particle board
1	1-1/2" x 3-1/2" x 8'	Yellow pine or Douglas fir (Stress-graded 2 x 4s)

Plumbing Fittings
1	1" x 5'	Galvanized pipe (threaded one end)
1	1" x 3/4"	Galvanized reducer coupling
1	3/4" x 2"	Galvanized nipple
1	3/4"	Galvanized Tee
1	1/2" x 11-1/2"	Galvanized pipe (threaded both ends)
4	1/2"	Galvanized pipe floor flanges
2	1/2" x 16"	Galvanized pipe (threaded both ends)
2	1/2"	Galvanized elbows
1	1/2" x 2"	Galvanized nipple

86

2	1" x 6"	Heavy-wall black boiler pipe (Schedule 80 XS) *Note:* When you have these two cut, request that the inside burrs on the cut ends not be reamed out.
1	1-1/4" x 30"	Galvanized pipe (optional)

Hardware and Supplies

4	No. 20	Worm-drive hose clamps (1-5/16" diameter)
2	No. 12	Worm-drive hose clamps (13/16" diameter)
3	No. 8 x 1-9/16"	Screw eyes
16	No. 10 x 3/4"	Flathead wood screws
48	No. 8 x 2"	Drywall screws
8	No. 8 x 1-1/4"	Drywall screws
1	12"	Flat rubber tie-down strap
1	15"	Flat rubber tie-down strap

Construction Procedure

1. Transfer the layout provided in Illustration 11 onto the 4' x 4' sheet of plywood or particle board. Double-check your measurements before cutting because the pieces are arranged on the board in a specific pattern. Don't worry about the rounded corners just yet; they'll be marked and cut in Step 4.

2. Put on your safety goggles and use a circular saw to cut out the nine pieces. Cut the single 48" centerline first in order to split the panel. Then cut the diagonal, followed by the two 24" cuts and the three 12" cuts. (The only two scrap pieces—the 5" x 6" pieces shown in the upper right-hand corner of Illustration 11—can be saved to place under your canvas, clay, and block when you're using the tile press.)

3. From the 8' 2 x 4, cut two 24" lengths and two 12" lengths. (You'll use the leftover piece to brace the lever out of harm's way; see Step 18.)

4. Lay out and trim the two side pieces, as shown in Illustration 12. (Save the 9" x 12" cutouts. One will be used to make the shimmed pad described in Step 15;

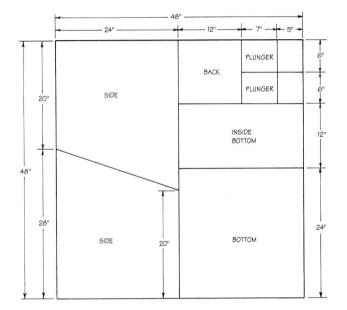

Illustration 11

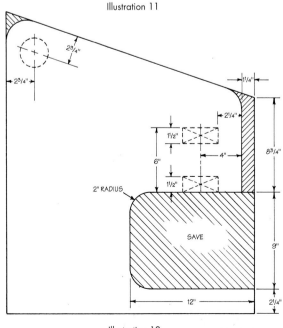

Illustration 12

George F. Fishman
Jubilee. 1989
32" x 48" (81.3 x 121.9 cm)

the other can be used to make pounding blocks for relief tiles.) Shape the rounded corners by tracing around the bottom of a 13-ounce coffee can; their radii are about 2". Note that the upper front edge of the press is first cut back by 1-1/4". On both sides of each side piece, mark the placement of the two 12" front cross supports; these positions are determined from the cut-back edge. The pipe-flange pivots at the rear are centered 2-3/4" from the rear and upper edges of the press; mark these positions on the inside face of each piece.

5. Place the 12" x 24" inside bottom section on top of the two 24" 2 x 4s so that the long edges are flush on both sides (see Illustration 13). Drill a series of 7/64" holes down each side, 5" apart and 2" in from the edges. Use the countersink bit to recess the hole openings. Then fasten the assembly with ten No. 8 x 2" drywall screws, using the power-drive bit in your drill.

Illustration 13). Mark for placement. Flip the whole thing over and draw two lines, each parallel to the 2 x 4s underneath and 7-1/2" in from an edge of the bottom section. Then drill another series of 7/64" holes, 5" apart, along these lines. Fasten the assembly to the bottom section by countersinking and fastening screws through these holes as before.

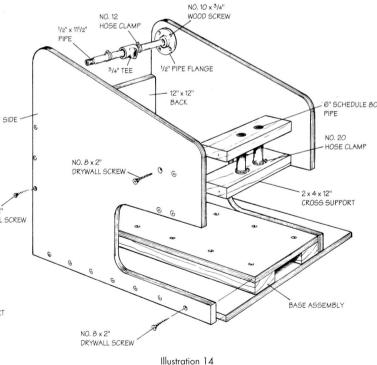

Illustration 14

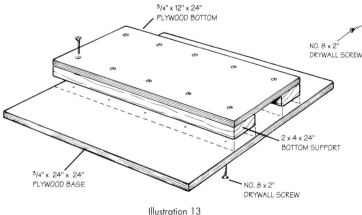

Illustration 13

6. Center this completed assembly on the 24" x 24" bottom section so that the lower board extends 6" from each side, and the front and back are flush (see

7. Fasten one of the two pipe flanges at the marked position on the inside of one side piece, using No. 10 x 3/4" screws (see Illustration 14). Mark the position for the other flange on the other side piece. Fasten it in place

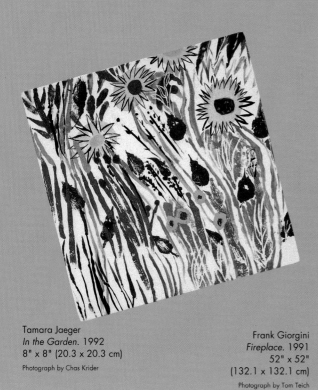

Tamara Jaeger
In the Garden. 1992
8" x 8" (20.3 x 20.3 cm)
Photograph by Chas Krider

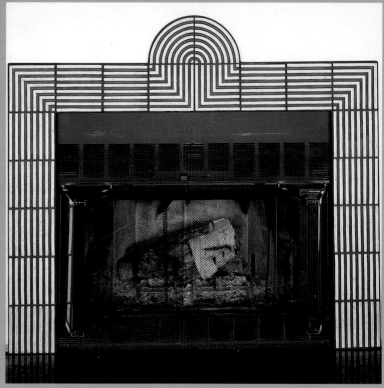

Frank Giorgini
Fireplace. 1991
52" x 52"
(132.1 x 132.1 cm)
Photograph by Tom Teich

with No. 10 x 3/4" screws and then unfasten it. (Creating the screw-holes in this manner will make final fastening easier.) Turn the base assembly upright and attach the side piece with the flange already on it to one edge of the inside bottom section, using seven No. 8 x 2" drywall screws along the side. Space the 7/64" holes 3" apart and countersink the openings as before.

8. Slip one No. 12 hose clamp onto the 11-1/2" section of 1/2" pipe, followed by the 3/4" Tee fitting and the other No. 12 clamp (see Illustration 15). Screw the pipe into the pipe flange that is fastened to the side piece and screw the other flange on the other end of the pipe. Then fasten the other side piece in place.

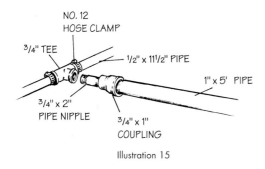

NO. 12
HOSE CLAMP

3/4" TEE

1/2" x 11 1/2" PIPE

1" x 5' PIPE

3/4" x 2"
PIPE NIPPLE

3/4" x 1"
COUPLING

Illustration 15

9. Position the 12" x 12" back section between the side pieces so that its lower edge is 7" above the base. Fasten it in the same manner as before, using three No. 8 x 2" drywall screws spaced 4" apart at each side. Check to see that the sides are perpendicular to the base. Thread the unfastened pipe flange in or out as needed to meet the side piece and then screw the flange in place.

10. Drill two 1-1/4" holes through both 12" cross supports, positioning the holes at the centerline of each

piece and centering them 3-1/2" apart (see Illustration 16). Enlarge the holes slightly with a round wood rasp until a length of 1" (I.D.) heavy-wall pipe fits snugly inside. Slip two No. 20 hose clamps onto each length of 6" heavy-wall pipe and tap the cross supports onto the pipe ends. Position and tighten the clamps so that they're against the inside faces of the two supports. (They may have to be readjusted later.)

11. Place the cross-support assembly between the side pieces at the positions previously marked. Drill two 7/64" holes through the sides and into the supports at each of the four marked joints. The holes should be 2" apart, and their faces should be countersunk. Fasten with eight No. 8 x 2" drywall screws.

CROSS SUPPORT

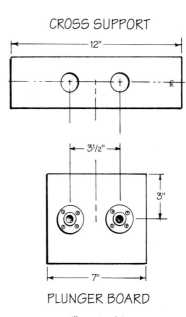

12"

3 1/2"

3"

7"

PLUNGER BOARD

Illustration 16

12. Assemble the plunger mechanism by threading the two 1/2" elbows onto the 1/2" x 2" nipple (see Illustration 17). Then thread the 1/2" x 16" pipes into the free ends of the elbows. Tighten the long pipes using two pipe wrenches—they both need to be the same length. Adjust the elbows on the nipple so that the pipes slip easily through the mounted cross-support pipe sleeves. Attach the pipe flanges after the plunger is installed and adjust them so that they're level.

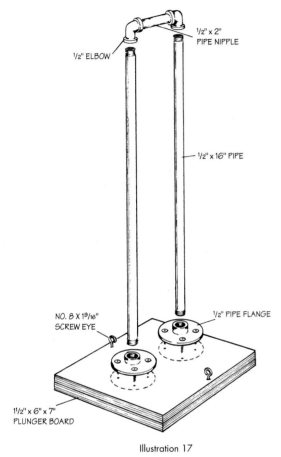

1/2" x 2" PIPE NIPPLE

1/2" ELBOW

1/2" x 16" PIPE

NO. 8 X 1⁹⁄₁₆" SCREW EYE

1/2" PIPE FLANGE

1¹⁄₂" x 6" x 7" PLUNGER BOARD

Illustration 17

13. Fasten the two 6" x 7" pieces together using four No. 8 x 1-1/4" drywall screws at the corners. The holes should be drilled with a 7/64" bit and countersunk. Then center the board beneath the two plunger flanges, with the 7" edge facing the front, and mark the eight flange screw holes. Remove the board, drill the mounting holes, and fasten the board to the flanges with eight No. 10 x 3/4" wood screws.

14. Use a 7/64" bit to drill two holes in the top of the plunger board, centered near the front and rear edges. Drill a third hole, centered in the back piece of the press. Fasten a No. 8 x 1-9/16" screw eye into each of these holes. Hook the 15" rubber strap into the eye at the front of the plunger board, run it up and over the top cross support between the two plunger pipes, and pull it down to hook the eye between that rear hook and the one fastened to the back of the press (see Illustration 18).

15. Because the plunger mechanism has some free play within the pipe sleeves, the 12" strap keeps the plunger board tilted slightly forward at a consistent angle. To compensate for this minute angle, you may

want to take the remaining 9" x 12" side cutout and mount its front corners to the front of the inside bottom section, so that it's directly beneath the plunger board. (Use No. 8 x 1-1/4" screws.) Then, by shimming up the rear of that pad with flat washers or metal or wooden shims, you can make its face parallel to that of the plunger board for a perfectly even pressing surface. Fasten the rear corners, too, once the proper angle is established.

16. To assemble the plunger lever, tighten the 1" to 3/4" reducer coupling onto the 5' length of 1" pipe (see Illustration 15). Then fasten the 3/4" x 2" nipple onto the reducer. Tighten this entire assembly into the end of the 3/4" Tee at the top of the press. Tighten the two No. 12 hose clamps at each side of the Tee fitting. The 5' lever arm rests on top of the plunger mechanism and provides leveraged pressure. If you're strong and plan to bear down on the arm for extra pressure, slip a 30" length of 1-1/4" pipe over the 1" by 5' lever arm to prevent the handle from bending.

17. Use some sandpaper and a block of wood to go over the press and remove any splintered rough edges. You can coat the whole press with polyurethane but doing so isn't necessary.

18. To protect yourself from accidental bruises, wrap the end of the lever arm with foam rubber and fasten it with attention-grabbing red tape. If possible, suspend a piece of rope with a loop in one end from the ceiling; use the loop to keep the lever arm raised and out of harm's way. Another way to keep the lever arm above eye level is to place a board (the 2 x 4 scrap left over from this project will work well) across the top of the press so that the lever arm rests on the board instead of on the cross-supports. Fasten two screws into the top edges of the side pieces to keep the board from sliding off. When the press isn't being used, unscrew the lever arm completely and store it in a safe place.

SIDE SECTION

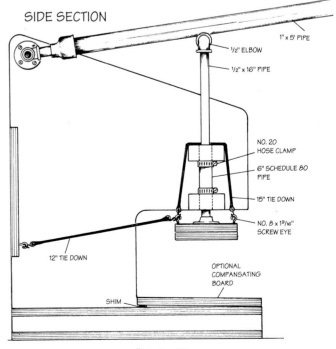

1" x 5' PIPE

1/2" ELBOW

1/2" x 16" PIPE

NO. 20 HOSE CLAMP

6" SCHEDULE 80 PIPE

15" TIE DOWN

NO. 8 x 1⁹⁄₁₆" SCREW EYE

12" TIE DOWN

OPTIONAL COMPENSATING BOARD

SHIM

Illustration 18

CHAPTER FIFTEEN

THE DAY OF ONE HUNDRED TILES

Frank Giorgini
*Tile Heritage Foundation
Commemorative Tile.* 1993
6" x 3" (15.2 x 7.6 cm)
Photograph by Bobby Hansson

As I was writing this book, I took on a large tile assignment from the Tile Heritage Foundation (a national, non-profit organization that provides information and referrals regarding historic and contemporary tile). This assignment was to design and produce a commemorative tile and to make six hundred replicas of it (Photo 87). I completed this task with help volunteered by friends and by students at Parsons School of Design in New York City. The finished tile is shown on the previous page.

87

As the project progressed, we learned how to improve our efficiency and production quality, and I also developed several new tools and techniques that helped to shove minutes—even hours—off production time. By the time the project was nearing completion, I was able to press out one hundred tiles, by myself, in a single day. For anyone who is considering a project of this magnitude, the technical information and time estimates that follow should prove quite valuable. Tiles as commemorative gifts, advertising hand-outs, awards, and coasters are a very feasible outlet for your tile designs and hand-production capabilities.

I'd been asked to design a 3" x 6" (7.6 cm x 15.2 cm) tile with *1992* and the Tile Heritage Foundation logo on it. The design that I came up with was a "tile on a tile," with

one of my stylized lizards holding on in the background; the foreground bore the logo and date. I envisioned this tile as carved bold relief, hand-pressed, fired to medium stoneware cone 6 in electric oxidation, with a matte-green Toshika glaze that I often use, one that breaks nicely over textured surfaces and has an old look to it. This design was approved.

I rolled out a 4" x 8" x 1/2" (10.2 cm x 20.3 cm x 1.3 cm) slab of moist clay and calculated shrinkage to obtain a final fired size of 3" x 6" (7.6 cm x 15.2 cm). I cut the slab down to the model size of 3-3/8" x 6-3/4" (8.6 cm x 17.1 cm) and drew my design roughly on it with a pin. By adding and scraping away clay, I slowly sculpted the surface into shape. I was meticulous about avoiding undercuts; I knew I had to produce many tiles from the mold, and I wanted them to release as easily and as quickly as possible.

In order to make twenty identical molds, I first prepared the forms and poured one mold. Then I produced nineteen more tiles with this mold, and as each one came out, I immediately made another mold from it (Photo 88). The second generation molds had to be made right away, before the tile models had a chance to shrink significantly. I kept the molds loosely stacked in front of the fan for five days because I knew that the

88

Opposite page, both: Lynda Curtis
Yirkalla II. 1993
Image: 16" x 16"
(40.6 x 40.6 cm)
Photograph by Bobby Hansson

Right: Randy Fein
Classical Dream. 1989
24" x 27" x 4" (61.0 x 68.6 x 10.2 cm)

Below: Bonnie Johnson
Journey. 1986
38" x 38" x 8" (96.5 x 96.5 x 20.3 cm)
Photograph by Steve duFour

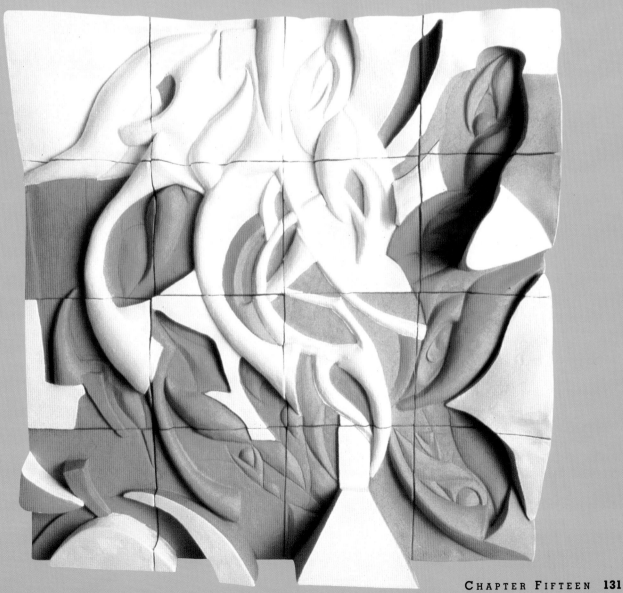

Peter Sohngen
Hex (detail). 1989
Overall: 24" x 15-1/2"
(61.0 x 39.4 cm)

drier they were, the faster we could pop out the tiles.

Next, we prepared twenty 3-3/8" x 6-3/4" x 3/4" (8.6 cm x 17.1 cm x 1.9 cm) clay plugs. At first, making these plugs was the most time-consuming step in the process. We were slicing off a slab of clay, pounding it flat with our hands, tracing a template, and then cutting each 3-3/8" x 6-3/4" (8.6 cm x 17.1 cm) shape. To save time, we tried rolling out a large, 3/4"-thick (1.9 cm) slab on the slab roller and cutting the shapes out of that. This method proved a little quicker, but it still took more time than we wanted to spend.

This was the point at which I invented the slab cutter described on pages 48 and 122-123. By using this tool, I was able to cut twenty 3/4"-thick (1.9 cm) tile-sized slabs really quickly. I then traced a 3-3/8" x 6-3/8" (8.6 cm x 16.2 cm) template on each slab and removed and wedged up the trimmings. The plugs were stacked with pieces of canvas between them, and the whole stack was covered with plastic. I could get twenty clay plugs from one 25-pound (11.4 kg) bag of clay, and after pressing the twenty tiles, we recovered about 13 pounds (5.9 kg) of clay.

I arranged my tools and work area so that everything I needed was close at hand: a piece of cardboard on which to place the plaster mold, a soft brush, a piece of canvas, a cut-off wire, a wooden straightedge, a rubber logo stamp, and of course, the Giorgini Studio Tile Press.

The next steps had a rhythm of their own. I took a mold from the stack in front of the fan and brushed out any dry clay or dust with the brush. Then I placed the mold face up on the cardboard, took a prepared clay plug from the plastic-covered supply, and patted it down into the mold opening. I placed the canvas and a wooden block over it, positioned the mold under the plunger of the tile press, pulled down the lever, turned the mold around 180°, and pulled down the lever again. Next, I removed the mold from the press, drew the cut-off wire across it, and placed the wadded-up trimmings into the plastic bag. I drew a straightedge across the top of the mold until the back of the tile was level and pressed in the logo. Finally, I removed the mold and placed it in the stack of molds to dry.

In less than one hour, the tiles were ready to pop out. I removed a mold from the stack, positioned it face up on the table, placed two sticks on it—one on each side of the opening—and then covered the sticks with a board. When I flipped the whole assembly over and tapped the board

on the table, the tile fell right out onto the board. I lifted the mold and stacked it with the others in front of the fan. Finally, I slid the tile off the board and onto a piece of wallboard large enough to hold twenty tiles.

Bisque firing, glazing, and glaze firing proceeded much as they're described in this book. In Chart II, you'll find suggestions as to how much time you might allow for each step of the entire process.

Chart II

Process	Allocated Time
Sculpting the model	2 weeks
Preparing 20 clay plugs	20 minutes
Pressing out 20 tiles with the studio press	40 minutes
Popping 20 tiles out of the molds and stacking the molds	20 minutes
Drying time (uncovered)	4 to 7 days
Loading 150 bone-dry tiles in electric kiln for bisque firing at cone 05	1 hour
Cone 05 bisque firing	13 hours
Cooling in the kiln	15 hours
Waxing the sides and back of 100 tiles	1.5 hours
Dipping 100 tiles in glaze and cleaning wax from backs and sides	3.5 hours
Loading 100 tiles into kiln for glaze firing	1.5 hours
Cone 06 glaze firing	13 hours
Cooling in the kiln	15 hours
Unloading the kiln	1 hour

CHAPTER SIXTEEN

HEALTH AND SAFETY

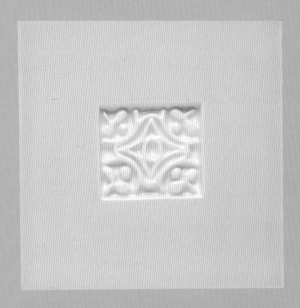

Emily Goodman
Sweet Peas, Abstract, Pig, and Coffee Cup. 1990
Each 5-7/8" x 5-7/8" (14.9 x 14.9 cm)
Photograph by David F. Mansure © 1993

Even for the beginning tile maker, safety and health should be primary considerations, so read this section carefully. For more detailed information, I would strongly recommend that you pick up a copy of *The Artist's Complete Health and Safety Guide* by Monona Rossol. This comprehensive text, though written for professional artists, provides accurate and easy-to-read information on the potential health hazards faced by all ceramists—and thoroughly explains how to avoid them.

The two primary concerns that you will have if you're working at home are the nature of the materials that you'll be using and the firing process. Clays, underglazes, glazes, oxides, and stains may all contain health-hazardous substances. When they're fired, they may also release dangerous gases, vapors, and fumes.

The following guidelines are distilled from Ms. Rossol's text. As well as following them closely, you should also request lists of ingredients from your suppliers for every substance that you use, in order to find out which ingredients are toxic. Ms. Rossol's text includes tables that will answer any questions you may have regarding these ingredients.

Home Studios

The best home-studio is the one that isn't a part of the home at all; it should be located in a shed or garage or in a basement that has its own entrance. This separation will help to keep air-borne dust particles, gases, and fumes out of your living space.

If you must work in your home, be sure that the space you choose is kept completely closed off from the rest of the house and is used for no other purpose. Work only with clays (not glazes) in that space and avoid dusty processes such as mixing glazes, sanding greenware, and reprocessing clay. (If you plan to create dust, work outdoors instead.)

If it's given a chance, clay dust will hitch a ride on your shoes, clothing, or body. Don't let it. Get a set of protective work clothes (avoid flammable synthetic fabrics) and a pair of shoes; when you leave the studio, wash up and leave them behind.

Cleanliness

Keeping yourself and your studio clean is especially important. Wash your work clothing frequently, keeping it separate from all other clothing. After working with glazes or underglazes, wash your hands carefully, using a nail brush when you do—and always wash up before you leave the studio.

Whenever you can, work "wet" and clean "wet." The less you move dust around, the better. Plan your work area with clean-up procedures in mind. Seal the floors and make sure that they're waterproof. Make or purchase tables, shelving, and equipment that can be sponged clean—and then sponge them clean when they need it. Wipe up spills right away. Clean compulsively!

Tools and Equipment

Keep all your tools and equipment in good condition. Because you'll be working with water, pay particular attention to the electrical condition of these tools and to the condition of your home or workshop wiring.

Kilns

Kilns can be hazardous on two fronts: fire in any form is a danger, of course, and your tiles—as well as the substances on them—can emit dangerous chemicals during the firing process. If you're a beginner, don't construct a kiln of your own. Handmade kilns are definitely not a project to undertake until you are an expert. And don't fire anything in your kiln unless you've had a proper ventilation system installed.

Electric kilns should be equipped with canopy hoods and negative pressure ventilation systems or isolated in a separate room that is provided with very rapid dilution ventilation. Stacks on fuel-fired kilns should be tall enough to keep emissions from floating into areas where they're not wanted. Unless these kilns are located outdoors, they should also be equipped with canopy hoods to collect emissions and gases during firing techniques such as reduction firing.

The position of your kiln is also important. See chapter 2 for specifics on situating a small, electric test kiln.

Opposite page: Lynda Curtis
Condah Series (detail). 1993
Each 3" x 6" (7.6 x 15.2 cm)
Photograph by Bobby Hansson

Right: Bernadette Stillo
Unite As One. 1993
5-3/4" x 7-3/4"
(14.6 x 19.7 cm)
Photograph by Bobby Hansson

Studio Ventilation

Proper ventilation isn't as easy to provide as you might think. Simply putting an exhaust fan in a window has a drawback: every cubic foot (28,317 cc) of dusty air that you exhaust must be replaced by a cubic foot (28,317 cc) of clean air. In the summer, you'll be hot unless that clean air is cooled, and in the winter you'll be cold unless it's preheated. Installing an air-conditioner won't work because an exhaust fan draws in replacement air quicker than an air conditioner can cool it. If you can't afford to have an engineer design a ventilation system for your space, place a three-speed exhaust fan, with a range of roughly 200 to 2000 cubic feet. (5.66 to 56.6 cubic meters) per minute (CFM), in an open window, and make sure that there's a window or door opposite to that window, one that can be opened when the fan is operated.

Fire

Plan fire protection carefully. If you have a kiln, keep it well away from all combustible materials. Equip it with two shut-off mechanisms in case one fails. Even if you plan to do your firing elsewhere, keep suitable fire extinguishers on hand in your work space.

Body Protection

Wear infrared-blocking goggles when you look into a glowing kiln, asbestos-substitute gloves when handling hot objects, impact goggles when chipping, and a dust mask or respirator when appropriate. Make sure that the mask or respirator will do its job; a dust mask, for example, won't protect your lungs from gases or fumes. No mask or respirator will protect you from the by-products of a poorly ventilated kiln, so be sure that your kiln ventilation is good. And check with your doctor before using any mask or respirator. If you have asthma or a heart condition or if you're pregnant, a mask may do you more harm than good.

Keep broken skin from contact with clay or glazes. Apply a good emollient hand cream after washing your hands. If you have skin problems, wear surgical or plastic gloves while you work.

Avoid repetitive strain and lifting injuries. Make repetitive and/or forceful movements of the hands and arms in short bursts and take frequent breaks. Never work to the point of exhaustion or pain. Change positions frequently. When wedging clay, keep the wrists in a neutral or mid-joint position and use the weight of your body rather than just the muscles of the upper limbs. Maintain good posture, too. Store heavy bags of clay and other materials at heights that won't require bending your back when you lift. When you do lift something, keep your back straight and use the muscles in your legs.

For processes such as glaze-spraying and mixing powdered chemicals, be sure to provide local ventilation such as a spray booth.

Obtain *Material Safety Data Sheets* from your distributor, as well as mineral and chemical analyses on all the materials you use. Never use materials containing highly toxic ingredients such as lead and asbestos. Treat materials that contain over 1% free silica as toxic and provide ventilation and/or respiratory protection when using them. If you're not sure which ingredients are toxic, get a copy of Ms. Rossol's text and read it thoroughly.

Always be prepared to provide your physician with information about the chemicals you use as well as your work practices. Have a lung function test each time you have a physical exam. If you decide to use lead-containing frits, glazes, or other materials, arrange for regular blood lead tests. Keep a well-stocked first-aid kit in your work area.

Disposal

Dispose of all old clays and glazes and other waste materials in accordance with occupational and environmental protection regulations.

Bettina Elsner
Exotic Scene #1—
Banana Tree with Monkey. 1988
34" x 34" (86.4 x 86.4 cm)

Peter King and Marni Jaime
Palm Beach. 1993
126" x 78" (320.0 x 198.1 cm)

Photograph by Gary Langhammer

Peter King and Marni Jaime
Mayan Relics. 1993
70" x 70" (177.8 x 177.8 cm)

Photograph by Gary Langhammer

APPENDIXES

Appendix A

TEMPERATURE EQUIVALENTS FOR CONE-FIRING RANGES

ORTON STANDARD CONES

Cone No.	Bending Temp. Centigrade	Bending Temp. Fahrenheit
022	585	1085
021	595	1103
020	625	1157
019	630	1166
018	670	1238
017	720	1328
016	735	1355
015	770	1418
014	795	1463
013	825	1517
012	840	1544
011	875	1607
010	890	1634
09	930	1706
08	945	1733
07	975	1787
06	1005	1841
05	1030	1886
04	1050	1922
03	1080	1976
02	1095	2003
01	1110	2030
1	1125	2057
2	1135	2075
3	1145	2093
4	1165	2129
5	1180	2156
6	1190	2174
7	1210	2210
8	1225	2237
9	1250	2282
10	1260	2300

Appendix B

FLOW CHART OF TILE TECHNIQUES

Moist Clay
- Rolling out slabs
- Brush on slips and engobes
- Impressing
- Slip trailing
- Direct carving
- Pressing with open-face mold
- Pressing with carved plaster block

Leatherhard Clay
- Brushing on slips and engobes
- Incising
- Inlay
- Shellac resist
- Underglazes
- Sgraffiato
- Screenprinting with underglazes

Bone-Dry Clay
- Underglazes
- Shellac resist
- Sgraffiato
- Screenprinting with underglazes

Bisqued Clay
- Underglazes
- Screenprinting with underglazes
- Rubbing on stains
- Sgraffiato
- Glazes

Glazed Clay
- Overglazes
- Lusters
- Decals
- Installation and grouting
- Mounting

APPENDIXES

Appendix C

SLIP FORMULAS

All-Temperature White Slip; Cone 04 to Cone 10
For Wet to Leatherhard Clay

OM4 Ball Clay	25.0%
Ferro Frit (3124)	20.0%
Flint	20.0%
EPK Kaolin	12.5%
Calcinated Kaolin	12.5%
Talc	5.0%
Zircopax	5.0%
	100.0%

To color this white slip, add underglaze colors (judging proportions by eye) or commercial stains or oxides (1% to 15%).

Archie Bray Black Slip; Cone 04
For Wet to Leatherhard Clay

Red Art Clay	46.73%
OM4 Ball Clay	23.36%
Manganese Dioxide	14.02%
Black Stain	11.22%
Black Iron Oxide	4.67%
	100.00%

Appendix D

GLAZE FORMULAS

Low-Fire Glazes

Waxy Satin Majolica
Cone 04; Oxidation

Ferro Frit 3124	72.72%
Whiting	9.09%
Flint	4.55%
EPK	4.55%
Zircopax	9.09%
	100.00%

A good, base white glaze; breaks nicely over relief terra-cotta surface.

DeB's Squash
Cone 04; Oxidation

Flint	42.0%
Gerstley Borate	38.0%
Lithium Carbonate	10.0%
Nepheline Syenite	5.0%
EPK	5.0%
	100.0%

Add:
Red Crocus Martis 10.0%

Nice yellow squash or mustard color; breaks to maroon over terra cotta.

Medium-Fire Glaze

Toshika Green
Cone 6; Oxidation

Potash Feldspar	34.5%
Whiting	21.6%
EPK	13.0%
Cornwall Stone	17.2%
Zinc Oxide	10.3%
Copper Carbonate	1.7%
Bentonite	1.7%
	100.0%

Semi-matte surface; breaks nicely over textured surface. Color ranges from cool green to tan-, brown-, and olive-green, depending on application.

High-Fire Glazes

Charlie D. White
Stoneware Cone 10; Reduction

Nepheline Syenite	20.0%
F-4 Feldspar	20.0%
Flint	20.0%
Dolomite	15.0%
Talc	13.0%
Ball Clay	10.0%
Whiting	2.0%
	100.0%

Add:
Superpax 10.0%
Bentonite 1.0%

Matte white in color.

Lapis Blue
Cone 10; Reduction

Potash Feldspar	40.0%
Whiting	25.0%
Cornwall Stone	20.0%
EPK	15.0%
	100.0%

Add:
Bentonite 2.0%
Cobalt Carbonate 2.0%

Lapis-blue color. Matte surface; breaks nicely to green and gun-metal gray. Must be applied very thinly, or it's just too blue.

APPENDIXES

Appendix E

CONE 10 GLAZE REDUCTION FIRING

The general schedule that follows is for a 30 cu. ft. (.84 cu. meter) natural-gas, updraft kiln, with a damper and flue on top of the chamber. The kiln has two forced-air gas burners with air blowers to control the fuel and air mix.

- Load the kiln with your ware; the tiles should lie flat on the shelves and should not touch each other. Arrange the kiln shelves at staggered heights so that there will be a free flow of heat throughout the interior.

- Position cone packs so that they're visible through the peepholes. This kiln does not have an automatic kiln-sitter shutoff. It does have a *pyrometer* (an electric temperature gauge), but the kiln must be shut off manually when the appropriate cone has fallen.

- Start the kiln with both burners set on approximately 1/4 pound per sq. in. (1723.5 Pa s). Set the pressure and blowers on 30%-50%. The gas-to-air mixture is adjusted to maintain a transparent blue oxidation flame. This is a low setting that will cause the temperature in the kiln to rise at a steady rate of about 150°F (83.3°C) per hour for about ten to twelve hours. For this reason, the firing is often started in the evening. Ten to twelve hours later, when you have to control the reduction process manually, it will be daytime.

- The next stage is known as *body reduction* and takes place at cone 07 for one hour. In firing terminology, reduction refers to the taking (reducing) of oxygen from the metal oxides in the clay body and the glaze, thus affecting chemical and color changes in both. Body reduction should take place between cone 08 and cone 06. When cone 07 is bending, adjust the burners to reduce the flow of oxygen into the kiln's interior. Adjust the airflow to the burners to its lowest setting. Increase the flow of gas to about two pounds per sq. in. (13788 Pa s). Adjust and partly close the damper at the top of the kiln chamber to create enough back pressure to maintain a lick of flame on one of the lower peepholes. Care must be taken not to create so much back pressure that it interferes with the operation of the burners. Partly block off the burner ports if necessary. For a period of one hour, adjust and readjust these controls every fifteen minutes; try to maintain an opaque orange flame from the burners. Back pressure should cause a slight flame to emerge from an opened peephole, but you don't want black smoke. You will also need to maintain the temperature and to control the flow of air within the kiln chamber so that reduction is uniform.

- To return the kiln's interior to a neutral atmosphere, readjust the burners and damper to achieve a neutral flame (multicolored, slightly purple, and translucent) that will effect a temperature rise of about 100°F (55.6°C) per hour. Maintain this temperature rise until cone 8, about four to five hours.

- The glaze reduction stage is next. When cone 8 is down and cone 9 is bending, repeat the one-hour reduction process in the same manner as you did for the body reduction.

- Return to a neutral atmosphere. Readjust the burners so that the temperature rise is about 30°F to 50°F (16.7°C to 27.8°C) per hour. Continue for about two to four hours, up to cone 10.

- When cone 10 is down, the firing is finished. Shut down the burners, and close the top damper. If you fail to shut the damper, the kiln will cool too rapidly, and your ware will probably crack. The cooling-down process will probably take twenty-four hours. Do not open the peepholes until the temperature is below 900°F (482°C). Do not open the door, even slightly, until the temperature is below 400°F (204°C). Remove the ware when it is cool to the touch.

Index to Artists and Photo Contributors

Index to Artists and Photo Contributors

Opposite page: Frank Giorgini
Afro Tile. 1993
12" x 12" (30.5 x 30.5 cm)
Photograph by Bobby Hansson

Above: Frank Giorgini
Afro Tile. 1992
12" x 12" (30.5 x 30.5 cm)
Photograph by Bobby Hansson

RESOURCES

To locate suppliers in the United States, look under "ceramic supplies" and "silk screening" in your telephone directory, or have your reference librarian show you how to use the *Thomas Register of American Manufacturers*. The latter lists U.S. manufacturers and their addresses. Advertisements in ceramics magazines are also a good resource.

Organizations

Orton Firing Institute
P.O. Box 460
Westerville, OH 43081
(Bi-monthly publication—Firing Line; quarterly; newsletter; technical tips for studio artists)

Tile Council of America
P.O. Box 326
Princeton, NJ 08542
(Tile testing)

Tile Heritage Foundation
P.O. Box 1850
Healdsburg, CA 95448
(Bi-annual magazine—Tile Heritage)
(Quarterly newsletter—Flash Point)

Tiles & Architectural Ceramics Books
3 Browns Rise, Buckland Common, TRING
Herts, HP23 6NJ, England
(Free booklist on request)

Publications

Ceramics Monthly
Professional Publications, Inc.
1609 Northwest Blvd.
Columbus, Ohio 43212

Books on Pottery and Ceramics

Behrens, Richard. *Ceramic Glazemaking: Experimental Formulation and Glaze Recipes.* (A Ceramics Monthly Magazine Handbook). Columbus: Professional Publications, 1986.

—. *Glaze Projects: a Formulary of Leadless Glazes.* (A Ceramics Monthly Magazine Handbook). Columbus: Professional Publications, 1981.

Chaney, Charles and Stanley Skee. *Plaster Mold and Model Making.* New York: Prentice Hall Press, 1986.

Chappell, James. *The Potter's Complete Book of Clay and Glazes.* New York: Watson-Guptill Publications, 1977.

Frith, Donald E. *Mold Making for Ceramics.* Radnor, Pennsylvania: Chilton Book Company, 1985.

Hamer, Frank. *The Potter's Dictionary of Materials and Techniques.* New York: Watson-Guptill Publications, 1983.

Harvey, A. Reid. *Plaster of Paris Techniques from Scratch.* Northampton, MA: Attic, 1992.

Nelson, Glenn C. *Ceramics.* 3d. ed. New York: Holt, Rhinehart and Winston, 1971.

Olsen, Frederick. *The Kiln Book.* Radnor, PA: Chilton Book Company, 1983.

Rhodes, Daniel. *Clay and Glazes for the Potter.* Philadelphia: Chilton Book Company, 1973.

—. *Kilns: Design, Construction, and Operation.* Philadelphia, Chilton Book Company, 1968.

—. *Stoneware and Porcelain: The Art of High-Fired Pottery.* Radnor, PA: Chilton Book Company, 1959.

Riegger, Hal. *Raku: Art and Technique.* New York: Van Nostrand Reinhold, 1970.

Rossol, Monona. *The Artist's Complete Health and Safety Guide.* New York: Allworth Press, 1990.

Troy, Jack. *Salt-Glazed Ceramics.* New York: Watson-Guptill Publications, 1977.

ACKNOWLEDGEMENTS

I would like to thank Joseph A. Taylor, president of the Tile Heritage Foundation, for having written the chapter entitled "The Handcrafted Tradition in Tiles" and for having provided so many beautiful photographs to accompany it. His generosity and patience are as remarkable as the depth and breadth of his knowledge. Many thanks, also, to the following people, for their expertise and information.

Lynda Curtis: Sgraffiato (chapter 7)

George F. Fishman: Mosaic assembly and installation (chapter 11)

Richard Freudenberger: Giorgini Studio Tile Press (chapter 14)

DeBorah Goletz: Kiln-firing schedules (chapters 8 and 10 and Appendix E)

Reneé Habert and Jim Stonebraker: Computer design (chapter 12)

Sandra McLean and Robert Stratton: Screen printing (chapter 7)

Monona Rossol: Safety (chapter 16)

Arnon Zadok: Installation (chapter 13)

I am deeply grateful to Bobby Hansson (Leaping Beaver Studios, Box 1100, Rising Sun, MD 21911), who has been photographing my work for years and who is responsible for the beautiful and dynamic photos that document the tile-making process in this book. His enthusiasm and expertise have been integral to this project. Don Osby, of Page 1 Publications in Hendersonville, NC, did a great job with the illustrations. My thanks also go to the skilled and enthusiastic tile makers who generously submitted photographs of their work and to the people listed below, who contributed additional photography.

Chris Blanchett
Tiles & Architectural Ceramics Books
(Address under Resources, this page)

Fired Earth Tiles plc
Twyford Mill, Oxford Road, Adderbury
Banbury, Oxfordshire, OX17 3HP
England

Nilüfer Alpsar and Dr. Süleyman Bodur
Kalebodur Seramik Sanayi A.S.
Büyükdere Caddesi
P.K.: (P. Box) 154
80620 Levent-Istanbul
Turkey

José Luis Porcar
Instituto de Promoción Cerámica
Diputación Provincial
Plaza de las Aulas, 7
12001 Castellón, Spain

I am also indebted to my family, especially to my wife, Joyce, whose support and assistance were invaluable contributions to this project; to Gino Giorgini Sr., Jr., and III; to Sharon and Mitch at Jack D. Wolfe Co., Brooklyn, NY; to Dennis, Dot, and Mary at Northeast Ceramic Supply, Inc., Troy, NY; to the teachers, administrators, and students of Parsons School of Design, NY, who collectively make Parsons an environment for creativity in the ceramic arts; to Chris Rich, my editor, whose skill and good humor kept me on track and over the coals; to art director Kathleen Holmes, for her creativity and composure, and to publisher Rob Pulleyn, whose vision made it all happen.

METRIC CONVERSION CHARTS

Lengths

Inches	CM	Inches	CM
1/8	0.3	20	50.8
1/4	0.6	21	53.3
3/8	1.0	22	55.9
1/2	1.3	23	58.4
5/8	1.6	24	61.0
3/4	1.9	25	63.5
7/8	2.2	26	66.0
1	2.5	27	68.6
1-1/4	3.2	28	71.1
1-1/2	3.8	29	73.7
1-3/4	4.4	30	76.2
2	5.1	31	78.7
2-1/2	6.4	32	81.3
3	7.6	33	83.8
3-1/2	8.9	34	86.4
4	10.2	35	88.9
4-1/2	11.4	36	91.4
5	12.7	37	94.0
6	15.2	38	96.5
7	17.8	39	99.1
8	20.3	40	101.6
9	22.9	41	104.1
10	25.4	42	106.7
11	27.9	43	109.2
12	30.5	44	111.8
13	33.0	45	114.3
14	35.6	46	116.8
15	38.1	47	119.4
16	40.6	48	121.9
17	43.2	49	124.5
18	45.7	50	127.0
19	48.3		

Volumes

1 fluid ounce	29.6 ml
1 pint	.473 l
1 quart	.946 l
1 gallon	3.785 l

Weights

0.035 oz.	1 gram
1 oz.	28.4 gram
1 lb.	453.6 grams

Temperatures

To convert Celsius to Fahrenheit, multiply by 9, divide by 5, and add 32.

To convert Fahrenheit to Celsius, subtract 32, multiply by 5, and divide by 9.

INDEX

INDEX

RELATED TITLES

The Ceramic Design Book
A Gallery of Contemporary Work
Introduction by Val M. Cushing
$34.95 Hardback ($52.95 Can.), 192 pages, 550 color photos
ISBN 1-57990-058-5
Distributed by Random House

The Clay Lover's Guide to Making Molds
Designing · Making · Using
By Peirce Clayton
$24.95 Hardback ($36.95 Can.), 128 pages , 120 color photos,
175 b&w photos
ISBN 1-57990-022-4
Distributed by Random House

Handbuilt Ceramics
Pinching, Coiling, Extruding, Molding, Slip Casting, Slab Work
By Kathy Triplett
$24.95 Hardback ($36.95 Can.), 160 pages, 400 color photos
ISBN 1-887374-29-9
Distributed by Random House

Surface Decoration for Low-Fire Ceramics
By Lynn Peters
$27.50 Hardback ($39.95 Can.), 160 pages, 350 color illus.
ISBN 1-57990-089-5
Distributed by Random House

Wheel-Thrown Ceramics
Altering, Trimming, Adding, Finishing
By Don Davis
$27.50 Hardback ($39.95 Can.), 160 pages, 400 color photos
ISBN 1-57990-052-6
Distributed by Random House